A LIFE

OUTBOXED

UNCONTAINED

THE MODERN LEADER'S
PLAYBOOK FOR BUILDING
A CULTURE OF EXCELLENCE

MARTIN LUTHER WHITE

Outboxed: A Life Uncontained
Copyright ©**2025** by **Martin Luther White**

All rights reserved. No part of this publication may be reproduced, stored in a retrieval system, shared, or transmitted in any form or by any means—electronic, mechanical, photocopying, recording, or otherwise—without prior written permission from the publisher, except for brief quotations in reviews or analysis.

Published by:
The 1 and Only Publishing
4500 Forbes Blvd
Lanham, MD 20706
Email: info@the1andonlypublishing.com
Website: www.the1andonlypublishing.com

Editing & Interior/Exterior Design:
The 1 and Only Publishing

Scripture Citation Notice:
Scripture quotations from **Philippians 4:12-13** are from the **King James Version (KJV)** of the Bible, which is in the public domain.

ISBNs:
Paperback: 979-8-89741-037-8
eBook: 979-8-89741-038-5

The views and opinions expressed in this book are solely those of the author.

Printed in the United States of America.

*To Sue, who saw the man I could become long before I did.
For Ariel and Ashia, my living proof that beauty,
brilliance, and courage can coexist.*

CONTENTS

FOREWORD 1

PREFACE 7

CHAPTER 1:
LOSS OF CHILDHOOD... 11

CHAPTER 2:
LEADING THROUGH SCARCITY.. 19

CHAPTER 3:
INTO THE NAVY... 39

CHAPTER 4:
STUCK IN THE MIDDLE... 57

CHAPTER 5:
THE MAKING OF A CHIEF... 75

CHAPTER 6:
REINVENTION AND REDISCOVERY.................................. 93

CHAPTER 7:
NAVIGATING NEW POWER STRUCTURES.....................107

CHAPTER 8:
THE PERFECT STORM...119

CHAPTER 9:
LEAD LIKE BRUCE LEE...127

CHAPTER 10:
THE BIRTH OF OUTBOXED 141

CHAPTER 11:
THE LEADERSHIP LAB..159

CHAPTER 12:
LEGACY—A LIFE UNCONTAINED....................................181

FOREWORD

LEADERSHIP IS RARELY FORMED IN COMFORT. More often, it is shaped quietly through experience—through responsibility that arrives before confidence, through moments when expectations are imposed before opportunity is offered, and through decisions that test not only competence, but character. Long before titles or authority appear, leadership begins forming in how we respond to pressure, rejection, and responsibility.

In my own experience, leadership was not developed through instruction alone, but through moments when growth was required and guidance was scarce. I learned early that titles do not make leaders; circumstances do. Being placed in situations where others depended on my judgment forced me to confront my own assumptions about leadership and to understand that growth often begins where comfort ends.

"You'll never get accepted into the program."

Those words landed as my platoon commander handed my high school transcripts back to me and walked away. No guidance was offered. No alternative path was suggested. In that moment, I understood what it felt like to be placed inside a box—defined not by potential, but by past performance. I stood there angry, but more than that, determined not to let someone else decide the limits of my growth.

That same year, I applied for an officer commissioning program anyway. I was selected—not because the system reversed itself, but because one leader, Major Earl, saw value where others saw limitation and was willing to stand behind me. I completed college and was commissioned as a second lieutenant in the United States Marine Corps. That experience reinforced an enduring lesson: leadership development depends less on institutions and more on individuals willing to invest in people.

Years earlier, those instincts had been forming quietly. As the youngest of three children raised primarily by my mother, I learned responsibility through work rather than instruction. Summers spent doing unglamorous labor alongside a local handyman—cleaning toilets, clearing gutters, finishing jobs no one wanted—taught me the discipline of starting what needed to be done and finishing it well. I was not the strongest student academically, but I learned early that education mattered and that leaving potential undeveloped was its own kind of failure.

The Marine Corps appealed to me for the same reason. It was difficult. It demanded discipline. It forced growth. Even there, leadership lessons arrived in unexpected ways. As a Corporal leading Marines during wildfire operations near Wenatchee, Washington, I once left my team in frustration to report what I viewed as insubordination. My Staff Sergeant asked a question that stopped me cold: "So you left them in the middle of fighting a fire to come tell me this?" In that moment, I realized leadership is not about reacting from emotion or leaning on authority, but about remaining present, responsible, and focused on the mission and the people entrusted to you.

After more than thirty years of service, that understanding was tested again at the highest level. As a battalion commander, I faced decisions I knew would likely prevent further promotion—and they did. Before making that choice, I sought counsel from a former Staff Sergeant of mine, now Sergeant Major Ronald Green, who would later become the 18th Sergeant Major of the Marine Corps. After listening, he said simply, "You weren't raised to do the wrong thing. You were raised right. You've been 'Green' trained."

That affirmation mattered. The decision before me was not about advancement; it was about stewardship. It was about whether I would accept a mold that required actions I believed would ultimately harm Marines, government employees, contractors, and their families. I chose instead to serve the people entrusted to me, knowing the cost. Leadership, I learned, is not measured solely by how far one rises, but by what one is willing to protect when pressure to conform is greatest.

Experiences like these make one truth unmistakable: leadership is not formed in classrooms alone, nor perfected through promotion or position. It is shaped in moments of tension, rejection, responsibility, and conscience—often when the system offers no clear path forward. Too often, leaders are taught how to fit the mold rather than how to think, discern, and lead with integrity when the mold itself is flawed.

This is why *OUTBOXED: A Life Uncontained* is necessary. This book does not present leadership as a polished formula or a linear progression. Instead, it reveals leadership as it is actually lived—formed through adversity, missteps, faith, perseverance, and the refusal to be defined by someone else's limitations. It speaks to those who have felt constrained by expectations, categorized too early, or pressured to sacrifice their values in order to advance.

I have known Martin for more than twenty years. Our families have spent time together, and I have seen him lead personally, professionally, and spiritually. I can say without hesitation that the integrity reflected in this book is consistent with the man I have known.

I do not offer my endorsement lightly. After a lifetime spent in environments where leadership decisions carried real consequences for real people, I have learned to recognize the difference between insight that sounds good and wisdom that has been earned. *OUTBOXED: A Life Uncontained* falls firmly in the latter category. It affirms that leadership rooted in character, discernment, and stewardship will always outlast leadership driven by ambition alone.

Reading this book is not a passive exercise. It invites reflection, challenges assumptions, and asks readers to examine how their own experiences have shaped the way they lead. The stories are honest and, at times, uncomfortable—but they serve a purpose. They create space for clarity, perspective, and growth. The lessons are not left abstract; they are translated into practical frameworks that leaders can apply in real situations, whether they are leading a family, a team, or an organization.

This book is worth your time.

Read it carefully.

KURTIS SARGENT SR.

PREFACE

From an early age, I felt the pressure of the boxes—other people's expectations, categories, and assumptions. Growing up as the youngest of nine children, I often felt unseen, like my role had already been determined before I had the chance to define it. Teachers, coaches, and even family members tried to place me into boxes that didn't fit. What I eventually discovered, though, was that I wasn't afraid to stand alone. I wasn't afraid to test myself against myself. That discovery—my refusal to fit in—was actually a strength, and it became one of my earliest lessons in living *outboxed*.

In time, I learned that being an outsider would become my greatest advantage as a leader. It taught me perspective—to see what others overlooked and to ask questions others were afraid to ask. It pushed me to think differently, to listen deeply, and to learn how to move even when the system didn't make room for me. Those early years shaped an awareness that would later guide every decision I made:

you can't influence what you don't understand, and you can't understand what you're not willing to see.

At first, that difference felt like isolation. But looking back, I realize it was instruction. The moments I felt furthest from belonging were the very moments that taught me how to lead—how to start without a roadmap, how to rebuild when everything breaks, how to move people forward when there's no applause to chase.

As I grew older, I realized a truth: many of us, as adults, let the weight of other people's expectations become our cage. We want to try something new—switch careers, move to a new city, pick up a hobby, even write a book—but we let *starting stop us*. We say, "That's not me. I could never do that." We rehearse the lie long enough that it becomes true.

Living a life uncontained means refusing that lie. It means breaking the box you've been placed in—or worse, the one you've placed yourself in.

This book is for leaders—especially those who've never felt like they fit the mold. It's for anyone navigating work, faith, or identity and wondering how to lead without losing themselves in the process. On the surface, it reflects my refusal to live inside other people's categories, assumptions, or boundaries. But it also connects back to my faith, to a verse that has been a compass for my life: **Philippians 4:13.**

The Apostle Paul, writing to the church at Philippi, said:

> *"I know how to be abased, and I know how to abound. Everywhere and in all things, I have learned both to be full and to be hungry, both to abound and to suffer need. I can do all things through Christ who strengthens me."*

For me, that verse is not just about endurance—it's about identity. Paul is saying that no matter the situation—abundance or lack, triumph or hardship—through faith in God, we are not contained by our circumstances. We are not defined by the highs or the lows. That truth shaped my life.

That's what *Outboxed* means to me. It's not rebellion—it's revelation. Some people aren't meant to fit the system; they're meant to expand it. Leadership, at its best, builds beyond the boundaries of what's been done before. It's about seeing differently, serving deeply, and finishing faithfully.

If you've ever felt out of place, different, or unseen, you're in the right place. You were never meant to fit the mold. You were designed to shape it. You were built to build.

The *Outboxed* mindset didn't start in a boardroom or on a stage—it started in a big, noisy house where love and chaos lived side by side. That's where I first learned that leadership isn't about position; it's about perspective. The lessons began long before I knew what to call them—in moments that tested patience, faith, and identity. That's where the real story begins.

CHAPTER 1
LOSS OF CHILDHOOD

MY EARLIEST MEMORY IS OF BEING PASSED FROM one pair of arms to another in the pews of Bethel AME Church in Springfield, Massachusetts. I was three years old—too young to fully understand the moment, but old enough to sense the weight of grief in the room. The stained-glass windows filtered soft light across the wooden pews, and I remember the smell of polished wood mixed with the heavy perfume worn by the older women. I was being handed across laps, from sister to sister, as if I were too restless or too young to sit still. Only later did I realize: this was my father's funeral.

That moment became the pivot point of my childhood. My father, Jeffrey Leon White, died when I was just three years old. He was only thirty-eight himself, taken by cancer. I was the youngest of nine children, and his death changed everything for our family. My mother, Beverly Mildred White, was only thirty-seven at the time. She had married young—and together they had built a life that, in the 1950s and 60s, was something to be proud of.

Before my father's passing, we were considered "well-off." My dad was educated, one of the rare Black men of his era with an associate's degree. He was also one of the only Black supervisors at the local warehouse, Sweet Life Distribution Center. My mom, in her own words, was a trophy wife. She was beautiful—petite, barely a hundred pounds, dark-skinned, always put together—and she enjoyed the life he provided. They lived in a large eighteen-room house with a basement that doubled as a nightclub for entertaining. Summers were spent vacationing at Martha's Vineyard. Black celebrities and community leaders passed through our home. For nearly two decades, my parents lived as socialites, raising nine children in relative comfort and style.

But when my father died, the curtain fell.

FROM COMFORT TO POVERTY

My mother was not prepared for widowhood. She had never worked outside the home and had little understanding of our family's finances. Although my father left life insurance and some savings, opportunistic people took advantage of her inexperience. Before long, the money was gone.

What followed was a descent into poverty. The grand house became a drafty, crumbling burden. The oil tank sat empty through harsh Massachusetts winters. I remember coming home to find the lights cut off. I remember the smell of smoke in my clothes from nights spent huddled around the fireplace because we had no heat. Trips to Goodwill replaced summer vacations. Sometimes food came from the generosity of family friends. One man who serviced vending machines would bring us discarded sandwiches. Some were moldy, some edible. We ate what we could.

And yet, through all of this, my mother had one determination: to keep her family together. She refused to allow her nine children to be split up, even when relatives offered to take one or two. That stubborn insistence, while it came at a cost, gave me my earliest understanding of leadership: **leaders may not control the circumstances, but they can define the values that hold people together.**

FAMILY DYNAMICS

In a family of nine, survival created its own hierarchy. We were grouped loosely into three categories: the older girls (Lillian, Alvine, and Candyce), the middle children (Jeffrey and Beverly, who were twins, and Gwen), and the "babies" (Richard, Robyn, and me). My older sisters were like second mothers, especially after my father's death. They bore responsibilities beyond their years—cooking, disciplining, and guiding the rest of us.

As the youngest, I absorbed it all—the loss, the chaos, the resilience. I didn't always process it in healthy ways, but it shaped how I saw the world. Where others saw scarcity, I saw challenge. Where others might shrink, I learned to fight—sometimes literally, sometimes figuratively.

LEADERSHIP IN CHILDHOOD

Looking back, I see how those years planted seeds of leadership in me. Leadership, I learned, isn't always glamorous.

Sometimes it's your oldest sister working two jobs so her younger siblings can eat. Sometimes it's your mother making the hard decisions despite appearances, because pride won't keep you warm. Sometimes it's you—the youngest child—watching all of it and deciding that one day you'll never let your family, or your team, stand in the cold if you can help it.

Poverty didn't just strip us of things; it taught us values: resilience, pride in our name, loyalty to family, and the instinct to defend ourselves. Those values would later become the foundation of how I led teams in the Navy, in business, and in life.

FRAMEWORK: FIVE LESSONS FROM LOSS

1. **Continuity** – Leadership without succession crumbles when the leader is gone.
2. **Systems Over Success** – Build structures that last beyond personality.
3. **Servant Leadership** – True leadership is sacrifice for those who depend on you.
4. **Team Dynamics** – Subcultures form naturally; wise leaders work with them, not against them.
5. **Stewardship** – Guard resources as fiercely as vision; what you don't protect, someone else will take.

TOOL: The Legacy Continuity Map
PURPOSE: Ensure your mission continues even if you disappear tomorrow.
USE WHEN: You're leading a team, project, or organization that depends heavily on you.

THE TOOL (3 STEPS)

Step 1: Identify the Mission-Critical Core

- What must NOT break if you are gone?
- (Values, processes, relationships, money flow, decision points)

Step 2: Build the Redundancy Net

- Document the 3-5 systems, backups, or people required to keep the core alive.

Step 3: Appoint & Equip a Successor

- Who can carry the core without you?
- What training or access do they need?

Closing Anchor

Leadership isn't measured by how brightly you burn while you're present—it's measured by what remains when you're gone.

CHAPTER 1 PLAYBOOK
FROM SURVIVAL TO LEADERSHIP

These playbooks will appear at the end of every chapter. They translate lessons into practical tools you can use—whether you're leading a family, a team, or an entire organization.

1. RESILIENCE TRAINING

TOOL: Adversity Journal
Each week, write down one challenge you faced and how you responded. Then list one way you could respond better next time. Over time, this builds a personal library of resilience strategies.

ACTION STEP: Start with last week. What tested your patience, discipline, or focus? Write it down and extract the lesson.

2. OBSERVATIONAL LEADERSHIP

TOOL: The Silent Five
Before entering a new team or environment, spend five days primarily observing. Ask questions, watch dynamics, and learn who influences whom before making big changes.

ACTION STEP: In your current environment, choose one person you haven't truly studied. Spend the next week observing how they operate and what others respond to in them.

3. LEGACY PLANNING

TOOL: The Succession Question
Ask yourself quarterly: *If I left tomorrow, who could step into my role?*

If the answer is "no one," start coaching someone now.

ACTION STEP: Identify one person in your circle who could grow into a leadership role. This week, give them one responsibility you normally handle yourself.

4. SYSTEMS OVER PERSONALITY

TOOL: The Continuity Test
Write down the top three things you do that keep your team, family, or organization running. Then ask: *Could someone else do this if I documented the process?*

ACTION STEP: Pick one of those three tasks and create a simple how-to guide or checklist for it. Share it with someone who could learn to do it.

CHAPTER 2
LEADING THROUGH SCARCITY

I REMEMBER THE ROUTINE OF MY HOUSE WHEN I WAS younger. Everybody had a job—dishes, cooking, laundry, cleaning up. It didn't matter that I was the youngest. Even when I was too short to reach the sink, I had a wobbly stool I stood on—when it was my turn to cook, I cooked. When it was my turn to wash dishes, I washed dishes. There were no passes, no excuses, no "I forgot."

Dinner was on the table promptly at six o'clock. That wasn't just a goal—it was law. And if you weren't at that table on time, you learned the consequences quickly. The first thing to disappear from your plate would be the meat. Then the vegetables. Then the starch. By 6:30, there was nothing left but a clean plate and your hunger—and if it happened to be your night to do the dishes, you were still on the hook for them, full belly or not.

That's how it was. Fair, firm, and consistent. Nobody needed to raise their voice or lecture us about responsibility; the system handled that on its own.

Looking back, I realize my mother was teaching us something deeper than chores. She was teaching us structure in the middle of instability. We didn't always have money, and the world outside our front door wasn't always kind—but inside that house, there were rules, order, and accountability. It was her way of keeping the chaos from swallowing us whole.

Even then, I didn't know it, but I was learning leadership at the dinner table. I was learning what culture really meant—not slogans, not motivational posters, but the daily rhythm of expectations. You showed up. You did your part. You respected the process.

And maybe most importantly—you learned that showing up late didn't stop the world from moving forward.

That's a lesson that still sticks with me today. In business, in leadership, in life—if you don't show up on time and do your part, somebody else will take your spot. And when the opportunity is gone, it's gone. But you'll still have to deal with the consequences.

WHEN SCARCITY FORCED SACRIFICE

But structure alone couldn't shield us from the harsh realities of poverty. After my father died, money was always tight. Some winters were harder than others, and there was one winter in particular I'll never forget.

The oil tank in the basement sat empty. The furnace didn't run. We had no heat, and winter in Massachusetts doesn't ask for permission, it just comes. The cold crept into every corner of that house, biting at your fingers and toes, making it impossible to sleep without shivering.

My mother did what she had to do. She started burning furniture.

Not all at once. It wasn't dramatic or reckless. It was methodical. She'd drag a chair to the fireplace, break it down piece by piece, and feed it to the flames. When the chairs ran out, she moved to the tables. Then the dressers. One by one, the things we once sat on, ate from, or stored our clothes in became kindling.

I remember the smell—the thick, acrid smoke that clung to our clothes and hair. We'd go to school reeking of it. Other kids would wrinkle their noses and step back. Teachers would glance at us with pity or judgment, I couldn't always tell which. Shame became another layer we wore, heavier than any coat.

But we stayed warm. And we stayed together.

We were proud of our name—White. My siblings drilled that into me early. "Never let anyone disrespect you," my brothers would say. Pride was armor. Pride was identity. But poverty tested it daily.

Still, my mother fought to keep us together. Relatives offered to take in one or two children at a time, but she refused. "We stay as a family," she would say. That stubbornness cost us comfort, but it preserved our unity.

And in that unity, I saw a truth that would shape my leadership philosophy later: leaders protect the integrity of the group, even when splitting them up would be easier. My mother's decision to keep us under one roof, no matter how broken, showed me that leadership isn't always about efficiency—it's about loyalty and vision.

BETRAYAL AND BOUNDARIES

There was a point, many years after my father died, when my mother had an on-again, off-again boyfriend. For a long time, I thought he was one of the good ones. He had a steady job, was kind to my mother, and showed an interest in me and my siblings. He'd tell me I was smart, that I had potential. Back then, I didn't hear that very often.

He'd take the time to talk *to* me, not just *at* me like most adults would. He'd ask what I wanted to be when I grew up, what subjects I liked in school. He even helped me get into summer programs and little community activities that were supposed to "build character." Maybe they did. But what I remember most was how much I wanted his approval. He filled a space I didn't even know I had—the space where a father should've been.

Sometimes, he'd let me tag along when he worked side jobs. He'd let me sweep up, carry tools, or just hand him things while he fixed something. He'd give me a few dollars afterward, and I'd feel like I'd earned something real. For a kid who grew up with uncertainty, that felt like stability—like manhood in small doses.

For a while, I genuinely believed he cared about me, about us.

But as time went on, things shifted. My mother and he would argue more. He'd disappear for weeks, sometimes months, then come back like nothing happened. Even as a boy, I could feel that inconsistency. I didn't have the words for it then, but I knew something about it wasn't solid.

Then came the fire.

THE DAY THE HOUSE BURNED

I was ten years old when I stepped off the school bus and smelled smoke. Fire trucks screamed past, and instinct pulled me to follow. As I ran closer, my stomach twisted. The smoke wasn't coming from some distant house—it was coming from ours.

I stood on the sidewalk, frozen, as flames licked out the windows and swallowed the walls. Neighbors gathered, murmuring in pity, but I couldn't hear them. My house—my history—was turning to ash before my eyes.

When the flames died, so had the life we once knew. Clothes, family photos, remaining furniture—all gone. What hadn't burned was lost in the aftermath. Insurance didn't cover enough. My mother, already struggling with money, couldn't keep up with the taxes. Eventually, the city took the property.

And that's when I learned what betrayal truly looks like.

See, that same man—the one who once talked to me about being a man of integrity—ended up acquiring the property. Our property. The same house I grew up in. The same walls that still smelled like my father's cologne. The same rooms where my mother worked herself to the bone to hold on after he passed.

He bought it—cheaply, I later learned—through back taxes my mother couldn't pay. We were struggling to survive, and he turned our struggle into an opportunity for himself. He didn't offer to help us reclaim it. He didn't even talk to my mother about it. He just bought it and moved his own family in.

For a long time, I couldn't make sense of it. How do you reconcile someone who once built you up with being the same person who tears something so foundational away from you?

That was the ultimate form of betrayal. Not just because of what he did, but because of what it revealed—that not everyone who sees potential in you wants to see you win. Some just want proximity to your light until they can figure out how to own a piece of it.

That moment planted something in me. A sense of vigilance. A skepticism that I would later refine into discernment. Because in life—and especially in leadership—you learn that good intentions don't always mean good outcomes. People can clap for you while quietly plotting how to benefit from your success.

But I also learned something about myself. I learned that pain doesn't always have to harden you. Betrayal can either build a wall or build wisdom. And while that moment broke something in me for a while, it also sharpened me. It made me more intentional about the kind of leader, man, and mentor I wanted to become.

I promised myself that if I was ever in a position to influence others, I'd never take advantage of someone's vulnerability. I'd never exploit trust for personal gain. Leadership, I came to realize, isn't about being the smartest person in the room or the one with the best plan—it's about being the kind of person others can safely follow.

Because the truth is, there are two kinds of power: the kind that controls people, and the kind that cultivates them. One leaves scars; the other leaves a legacy.

And that day, watching that man move into what used to be my home, I decided which kind of power I wanted to carry.

Looking back, it was also stewardship I lost. Leadership

isn't only about guiding people—it's about guarding resources. My mother didn't have the tools to protect what she'd been entrusted with, and we paid the price. Leaders who fail to steward resources well don't just lose possessions; they lose trust, security, and, sometimes, legacy.

PILLAR TO POST

After the fire, we lived "pillar to post," bouncing between relatives and friends. I remember staying with my mother's suitor's mother—a woman who wasn't even family but took us in because she had space.

There's a humility in living off someone else's generosity, and it's not easy to swallow. For a boy who already felt the sting of shame from poverty, it was another reminder of what we'd lost. But it also reinforced something: communities matter. No one leads alone, no one survives alone. Even leaders need support systems—people willing to step in when life takes everything away.

MY MOTHER'S NIGHT SHIFTS

Amid all of this, my mother found work. She took a job at Sweet Life, the very warehouse where my father had been a supervisor. But she wasn't in his office; she was on the floor, hauling freight.

I can still picture her walking in late at night, exhausted, clothes damp from sweat and cold, too tired to cook but still asking us about our day. She was a small woman, barely over a hundred pounds, but she carried the weight of a family on her back.

At the time, I didn't call it leadership. I just saw a mother doing what had to be done. Now, I recognize it for what it was: servant leadership in its rawest form. She chose humiliation and hardship to keep us fed. She did the hard work—not for recognition, but for survival.

That image of her has never left me. It shaped my understanding of what it means to lead—not the speeches or the titles, but the willingness to work in the dark when no one is watching.

MA WHITE'S UNITED NATIONS HOUSE

I told you that my mom and dad used to entertain a lot when my father was alive. The house was always filled with people—neighbors, friends, cousins, even the occasional politician or local celebrity. But here's the thing: even after the house burned down, and even after years of scraping by, that atmosphere of openness didn't disappear.

When my mother finally started working steadily and we could afford to rent our own place, she recreated that same spirit. She used to say her house was the "United Nations." All were welcome, and that was literally what you saw on any given day. An eclectic group of kids and adults filled the rooms—ages ranging from toddlers barely old enough to walk to grown men and women in their forties who came through because of my Mother or my brothers and sisters. Since there was such a large gap between my oldest and youngest siblings, the friends they brought with them stretched across every generation.

And through it all, my mother was the same. Hospitable. Loving. Protective. She grew up in a time when Black people across the nation, faced real barriers—segregation, discrimination, limits on opportunity. But she never let that harden her. She wasn't bitter. She wasn't closed off. She loved everyone, and she welcomed everyone.

I can say this, not just through the lens of a child admiring his mother, but through the lens of someone who spent his whole life watching how people responded to her. My mother had a gift. She could take a room full of strangers and, within minutes, make them feel like family.

I remember coming home several times as a kid, thinking friends were there waiting for me, only to find out they weren't there for me at all. They were there for "Ma White." That's what everyone called her. She had that effect. Once she loved you, you were hers. She would fight for you, defend you, feed you, and fold you right into the family.

Even her language was inclusive. She never said "this is my son-in-law" or "that's my daughter-in-law." No. She said, "This is my son. This is my daughter." There was no qualifier. There was no second-tier status. Once you were in, you were in.

And what makes this even more remarkable is that we didn't have much. We didn't have the nicest furniture, the latest clothes, or fancy meals. But the food always stretched. The doors always stayed open. The atmosphere was always warm. People wanted to be in our house, not because of what we had, but because of how my mother made them feel. She created a safe place—a space where people could simply be themselves.

Looking back now, I realize that this was another form of leadership. Not the kind that comes with rank, titles, or authority—but the kind that comes with presence, love, and consistency. My mother modeled a truth that I carry with me today: the environment you create will always outlast the resources you have.

LEADERSHIP LESSONS IN THE FIRE

I didn't know it then, but this chapter of my life was another classroom. Poverty, fire, and resilience taught me leadership in ways no textbook ever could.

- **Adaptability:** Watching my mother burn our furniture showed me that leaders sometimes make painful sacrifices to survive.
- **Resilience under scarcity:** Eating stale sandwiches and wearing donated clothes built endurance. Leadership requires toughness born from scarcity.
- **Servant leadership:** Watching my mother work nights modeled sacrifice as a leadership style.
- **Stewardship:** Losing our home revealed the cost of failing to protect resources.
- **Team loyalty:** My mother's refusal to split us up proved that leadership means protecting the group's integrity, even when it's inconvenient.
- **Discernment:** Betrayal taught me to be vigilant about who I trust with power and proximity.
- **Environment over resources:** Ma White's United Nations showed me that culture outlasts comfort.

Those lessons burned into me as surely as the flames that consumed our house. They became the foundation of how

I would lead later in life: with adaptability, resilience, and loyalty—even when it meant sacrifice.

LEADING THROUGH SCARCITY

Scarcity strips leadership down to its rawest form. When resources vanish, appearances collapse, and pride feels empty, leaders must decide: *What will I sacrifice, and what will I protect?*

Framework: The Five Fires of Scarcity Leadership

1. **Adaptability:** Leaders sometimes make painful, even unthinkable sacrifices to keep the mission alive.
2. **Resilience Under Scarcity:** Hardship is a forge; it produces toughness if you stay in the fire.
3. **Servant Leadership:** True leadership means showing up when you're exhausted, even if no one is watching.
4. **Stewardship:** Leaders must guard resources. Losing what you've been entrusted with costs more than possessions: it costs trust and legacy.
5. **Team Loyalty:** Protecting unity matters more than protecting efficiency. Sometimes keeping the group together is the leadership win.

TOOL: The Scarcity Map

PURPOSE: Make fast, rational decisions when resources collapse.

USE WHEN: Budget cuts, reduced staff, crisis, loss of key resources.

THE TOOL (3 QUESTIONS)

1. What must be protected at all costs?

Name the essential mission.

2. What can be sacrificed without killing the mission?

Identify symbols, comforts, routines, or ego-driven tasks.

3. What limited resource must be stewarded most carefully?

Time, money, people, attention, relationships, energy.

Reflection: Check Yourself

- Do I cling to appearances at the expense of survival?
- When resources run low, do I panic—or adapt?
- Am I protecting the team's unity, or am I making decisions that fracture it?
- Where have I failed to steward resources well, and what did it cost?

ACTION: Write down your answers. That's your Scarcity Leadership Map—and it shows you both your strengths and your blind spots.

Closing Anchor

Leadership in scarcity isn't about keeping everything. It's about protecting what matters most, sacrificing what can be burned, and stewarding the rest so your people survive to fight another day.

LEADERSHIP PLAYBOOK
THE UNITED NATIONS OF LEADERSHIP

PURPOSE: Build culture by creating belonging, safety, and unity.

USE WHEN: You're leading a diverse team with mixed backgrounds, cultures, or personalities.

1. Radical Welcome Creates Loyalty

Just like Ma White's door was always open, great leaders create environments where people feel they belong, no matter their background.

APPLICATION: Begin meetings or team check-ins by asking about people, not just tasks. Make inclusivity a consistent, visible practice.

2. Titles Don't Define Relationships

She never said "in-law." She said, "my son, my daughter." That simple reframe erased distance and created instant belonging.

APPLICATION: In leadership, titles and roles matter for clarity, but relationship-building matters for culture. Learn names, learn stories, and use inclusive language that signals people are valued beyond their job description.

3. Resourcefulness Over Resources

Our family never had the newest furniture or the fanciest meals, but the food stretched, and the house felt full. People weren't drawn to things—they were drawn to love.

APPLICATION: Leaders often think they need more budget, more tools, or a bigger headcount. What they actually need is the ability to stretch what they have and make people feel secure, not restricted.

4. Protect Fiercely, Support Consistently

Once someone became family to my mother, she defended them like her own. That kind of loyalty can't be bought; it has to be demonstrated.

APPLICATION: Stand up for your team publicly. Correct and coach privately. Make it clear that anyone under your leadership is safe in your presence.

5. A Safe Place Is the Greatest Asset

People didn't flock to our house because it was the biggest or the nicest. They came because it was safe—emotionally, socially, spiritually.

APPLICATION: Create work environments where people don't fear humiliation or dismissal. A culture of safety drives risk-taking, creativity, and trust.

CHAPTER 2

PLAYBOOK LEADING THROUGH SCARCITY AND LOSS

1. RESILIENCE UNDER SCARCITY

TOOL: Scarcity Simulation Exercise

- Give your team a "limited resource" challenge—restrict budget, staff, or time on a small project.
- Debrief after: How did people feel? How did they prioritize?
- Discuss how to translate that resourcefulness into normal operations.

APPLICATION: Builds problem-solving skills and endurance for when real scarcity hits.

2. SERVANT LEADERSHIP IN ACTION

TOOL: The Shadow Exercise

- Spend one full day shadowing your frontline employees or team members.
- Do their work, experience their environment, feel their challenges.
- End the day by asking: What did I learn that I didn't know before?

APPLICATION: Reinforces humility and ensures leaders make decisions from empathy, not distance.

3. STEWARDSHIP OF RESOURCES

TOOL: Resource Risk Audit

- **Step 1:** List critical resources (finances, assets, intellectual property, customer trust).
- **Step 2:** For each, identify the biggest risks (neglect, poor planning, lack of oversight).
- **Step 3:** Assign clear accountability for stewardship.
- **Step 4:** Create a contingency plan for the top 2 risks.

APPLICATION: Prevents leaders from "losing the house" by failing to manage what they've been entrusted with.

4. PROTECTING TEAM LOYALTY

TOOL: Integrity Line Test

- Ask: What's the one thing I will never compromise to make life easier?
- Communicate that standard to your team.
- Revisit it quarterly to ensure decisions still align.

APPLICATION: Gives team members a clear sense of non-negotiables, strengthening trust during hard times.

5. COMMUNITY RELIANCE AND SUPPORT SYSTEMS

TOOL: Support Circle Mapping

- Identify 5-7 people or organizations who would step in during a crisis.
- Build those relationships proactively (don't wait until you need them).
- Offer value back to them regularly—support flows both ways.

APPLICATION: Leaders who invest in community resilience ensure survival when everything else burns down.

KEY TAKEAWAYS

- Scarcity isn't just survival—it's a leadership lab.
- Leaders must balance sacrifice, resource stewardship, and loyalty to their people.

- ◆ Servant leadership is most powerful when modeled in hardship.
- ◆ True resilience comes from both toughness and community reliance.
- ◆ The environment you create will always outlast the resources you have.

CHAPTER 3
INTO THE NAVY

With my mother working nights, I was left to my own devices. I learned to fight because I had to. My brothers drilled one rule into me: never let anyone disrespect you. I took that advice to heart. If someone even said they wanted to fight after school, I didn't wait. I struck first, hard, and often.

Violence became my answer to everything. And drinking wasn't far behind. My friends and I would pour half a two-liter Coke out, fill it with Bacardi, and drink it during the day like it was nothing. It became routine. By high school, I was more brawler than student.

By my senior year, I was expelled from every public high school in Massachusetts for fighting. My mother, with no other options, made the hardest choice she could: she sent me to Florida to live with my sister Beverly (we called her Missy).

Missy was Navy through and through. Structure. Discipline. She gave me one shot: graduate or fail out of life.

I didn't realize it then, but she and her husband Mike were saving me.

Even with Missy and Mike watching over me, I almost blew it. I had to pass all my classes to graduate on time, but in English class, I was one point short of a passing grade. When I asked my teacher—Mrs. Mumms, whose class I had been disruptive in all semester—for extra credit, she made me a deal for the extra point. I had to perform a scene from Macbeth in front of the class. Not just our class—she brought in another class to watch.

She handed me a curtain to use as a cape and a rod for a sword. "The drunken porter scene," she said.

Some might have found it humiliating. Me? I didn't care. I stood up, performed the scene, and earned the one point I needed. I graduated.

The second turning point of my life.

When I graduated high school at seventeen, it wasn't with honors or accolades. It was with relief—and with my sister standing right beside me. Missy was a Navy recruiter at the time, and looking back, I know she had this planned all along. She knew I needed structure, purpose, and a way out of the destructive cycle I had fallen into. The Navy became that way out.

Boarding that plane, I didn't know I was leaving one fire for another. It was 1987. The Cold War still defined global politics, and the Navy was a tough, uncompromising institution. Boot Camp wasn't built to nurture—and for someone like me, stubborn and hot-headed, it was exactly the shock I needed.

BOOT CAMP: THE MAKING OF A SAILOR

I remember Boot Camp vividly. It was a cold September in Chicago—September 9, 1987—and I was just a kid trying to figure life out. Boot Camp back then wasn't like it is today. It was designed to break you down to the studs and rebuild you into something the Navy could depend on. It didn't matter who you were back home—once you stepped through those gates, you were just another recruit with a head full of uncertainty and your name stenciled on your chest.

My two Company Commanders were Chief Reyes and Petty Officer Meyer. I remember them both vividly, for very different reasons. Petty Officer Meyer was a short, stocky dude with a mustache that looked like it had been drawn on. He carried himself like he was ten feet tall, though, and he made sure you felt it. He was the kind of man who didn't need to raise his voice—his presence did all the talking.

I had a bit of a smart mouth back then, and thought I was slick. My sister had been a recruiter, so I figured I knew the ropes. I didn't. I didn't know the difference between a Chief and a Petty Officer, didn't understand rank or the subtle art of military respect. To me, it all seemed like costumes and commands. And to Meyer, that made me the perfect project.

He seemed to have a sixth sense for my sarcasm. If I rolled my eyes or whispered under my breath, I'd find myself doing push-ups until the floor sweated beneath me. His favorite punishment was to make me hold the "front-leaning rest position"—down on my hands, body shaking—while he lectured the rest of the company. He'd say "Down," wait four or five seconds, then finally say "Up," like he was savoring the delay.

After a while, my arms stopped trembling. Somewhere between punishment and repetition, my body toughened up. I learned that endurance isn't built in comfort. It's built under pressure, in the quiet burn of effort, where no one applauds.

Chief Reyes was the opposite in almost every way. Tall, olive-skinned, and full of charm, he carried himself like the main character in his own movie. He was proud—too proud sometimes—and fancied himself a ladies' man. That became obvious the day he introduced the "Sweetheart Board."

It was a corkboard at the entrance to the barracks where recruits could pin pictures of their girlfriends, wives, or whoever was waiting for them back home. At first, it seemed harmless—something to remind you of why you were there, what you were working for. Guys would stop by the board and stare for a few seconds before lights out, maybe draw a little strength from it.

But Chief Reyes had a different purpose for it.

During the final week of Boot Camp, he started going down the line, pointing at pictures and asking, "Who does she belong to?" When a recruit raised his hand, the Chief would smirk and say, "Good. You'll be on watch during graduation." He'd then add, with that same grin, "Don't worry—I'll keep her company."

He'd tell us that's what "Jody" does when you're out to sea—Jody being the mythical man back home who takes your girl while you're gone. It was crude humor, maybe even cruel humor, but in its own twisted way, it was another lesson about life and leadership: control what you can, accept what you can't, and understand that perception—whether true or not—shapes morale.

At the time, I laughed. Mostly because I didn't have a girlfriend, so I was off the hook. But that moment stuck with me. Even in his mockery, Chief Reyes was teaching something about the balance between leadership and manipulation. He knew how to command attention, even if it was through fear or discomfort.

Meyer taught me endurance. Reyes taught me psychology.

Between the two of them, I began to understand something I would carry for the rest of my life: leadership isn't about barking orders—it's about knowing how people work. How they think, react, and respond under pressure.

Looking back, Boot Camp was more than just a military indoctrination. It was the first time I saw how systems create order, how structure drives performance, and how personalities—flawed or not—can shape entire teams.

Those early weeks in Great Lakes weren't just about learning how to march or salute. They were my introduction to the deeper layers of leadership—the kind that lives between discipline and empathy, control and chaos.

And even though I couldn't see it then, that was the first time I began to outgrow the boy who washed dishes on a wobbly stool.

BOOT CAMP AND BEYOND

At first, I thought I had the system figured out. I was smart enough to test into one of the top Navy schools for electronics. On paper, I had a future as an electronics technician—one of the most prestigious enlisted roles. But pride and arrogance got the better of me. I didn't want to sit in classrooms. I didn't want to study. I wanted action. So I did what I had always done when I didn't want to play by the rules—I found a way to get kicked out.

That decision changed my trajectory. Instead of a technical path, I ended up as an "undesignated seaman"—the Navy's way of saying, "You'll do whatever we need until you prove yourself useful."

It wasn't glamorous. It was paint, grease, sweeping decks, and grunt work. But it was also the beginning of my education in leadership.

THE FIRST FIGHT AT SEA

My first ship was the USS Forrestal, an old conventional aircraft carrier stationed out of Mayport, Florida. The day I arrived, I was dropped off in the berthing compartment—rows of bunks stacked three high, with a small lounge off to the side. I sat in one of the chairs in the lounge, waiting for the rest of the division to return from work.

When they did, a sailor named John walked in, looked at me, and said, "You're in my seat."

There were a dozen empty seats in the room, but he wanted mine. I ignored him at first. Then he said it again, louder. Finally, he reached to pull the chair out from under me.

That was it. Instinct took over. I jumped up, and we fought right there in the lounge. No words, just fists. The rest of the sailors didn't stop us—they watched, laughing, waiting to see what I was made of. After a few minutes, they pulled us apart. One of them grinned and said, "Welcome to deck department."

That was my introduction to Navy life. Fitting, in a way. I had been kicked out of high school for fighting, and the first thing I did in the Navy was fight. But what I didn't realize then was that the fight wasn't just about dominance—it was a test of resilience. In their eyes, I had passed.

LEARNING THE SAILOR'S TRADE

Assigned as a boatswain's mate, I learned the traditional skills of seamanship. Chipping paint, splicing line, working on deck during refueling, and driving small boats. It was hard, dirty, physical work. But it also carried responsibility. As a junior sailor, I was put in charge of small crews performing specific tasks.

It was my first taste of leading people formally. I didn't have the rank, but I had responsibility. I learned that if I didn't give clear instructions, mistakes could be dangerous—even fatal. That was the first time I saw that leadership isn't about power; it's about clarity and accountability.

MARRIAGE AND FATHERHOOD

During that first enlistment, I also got married—to the woman who remains my wife to this day. We had our first child, and suddenly the stakes felt even higher. It wasn't just about me anymore. It was about providing for our family.

But I was still young, still stubborn, still prone to fighting in bars on liberty. My wife made me promise to stop. I tried—but it took years before I really learned how to replace my fists with words.

OPPORTUNITIES MISSED

Around this time, the Navy rolled out a program to diversify its officer ranks. Sailors with strong test scores and certain demographics were invited to apply for a path to Officer Candidate School. I received one of those invitations.

My chain of command encouraged me to apply. They saw potential. But I refused. I didn't want the responsibility. I didn't believe I'd be in the Navy long enough to make it worthwhile. So I passed on the opportunity.

It's a decision I regretted for the rest of my career. I spent twenty-six years chasing advancement, always just shy of becoming an officer. That letter had been my chance—but I was too short-sighted to see it.

That was one of my earliest leadership lessons: sometimes the opportunity you ignore becomes the regret you carry.

THE WEIGHT OF DEPLOYMENT

In those first years, I made my first deployments—long months at sea, with only steel decks and endless ocean as company. I learned what it meant to live in close quarters with thousands of sailors, to endure monotony, to find routine in chaos.

Deployment taught me that leadership isn't always about big decisions; sometimes it's about consistency. It's about showing up, day after day, being steady in the storm.

SEEDS OF LEADERSHIP

Even as I stumbled through those years—fighting too much, missing opportunities, learning the hard way—I was being shaped. The Navy of the late 1980s was tough, uncompromising, and often unforgiving. It didn't bend to you—you bent to it.

And in that crucible, I started to see the leader I could become. Not polished, not refined, but resilient, decisive, and slowly learning that leadership wasn't about proving toughness—it was about creating trust.

LESSONS FROM THE DECKPLATES

From those early Navy years, I carry these lessons:

1. **Respect is earned in the arena**. The fight with John wasn't about violence—it was about showing I could stand my ground. Leaders earn respect by showing they belong.
2. **Clarity saves lives**. Giving clear instructions while leading deck crews taught me the power of communication.
3. **Opportunities don't knock twice**. Passing on the officer program taught me the cost of short-sighted decisions.
4. **Consistency is leadership**. Deployment showed me that being steady, day after day, builds trust more than bursts of brilliance.
5. **Leadership grows from mistakes**. Every fight, every misstep, every missed chance was a lesson shaping me into a better leader.

6. **Endurance is built under pressure**. Meyer's push-ups taught me that toughness comes from repetition and resilience.
7. **Psychology matters as much as tactics**. Reyes showed me that understanding how people think is as important as what you tell them to do.

THE FRAMEWORK: FOUNDATIONS OF TRUST

Early leadership isn't about authority—it's about credibility. In environments like the Navy (or any high-stakes organization), people decide whether to follow you long before you have a title.

Foundations of Trust rest on four anchors:

1. **Respect is Earned in Action**—People don't trust talk; they trust consistency.
2. **Clarity Prevents Chaos**—In complex work, clear instructions are life or death.
3. **Opportunity Costs**—The chances you ignore today often define tomorrow.
4. **Consistency Builds Credibility**—Showing up steadily matters more than showing up perfectly.

THE TRUST COMPASS

PURPOSE: Build trust quickly when entering any new environment.

USE WHEN: New job, new team, new role, new project.

THE FOUR BEARINGS

1. **Respect** – How are you showing people they matter?
2. **Clarity** – Are you removing confusion before it begins?
3. **Consistency** – Can people predict your behavior?
4. **Choices** – Are you saying YES/NO to the right things?

Weekly Use

- Set one action for each bearing on Monday
- Review alignment on Friday

CHAPTER 3
PLAYBOOK TURNING CHAOS INTO DISCIPLINE

THIS PLAYBOOK TRANSLATES THE LESSONS OF MY early Navy years into practical tools leaders can use to channel energy, face adversity, and seize opportunities.

1. CHANNELING RAW ENERGY

TOOL: The Redirect Framework

- **Step 1:** Identify your "default reaction" under stress (fight, freeze, over-control, withdraw, etc.).
- **Step 2:** Write down 2–3 productive alternatives you can train yourself to use (e.g., ask a clarifying question, take a pause, delegate).
- **Step 3:** Practice in low-stakes situations so it becomes a reflex.
- **Step 4:** Use an accountability partner to call you out when you slip into old habits.

APPLICATION: Helps leaders harness passion without letting it become destructive.

2. LEARNING THROUGH HUMILITY

TOOL: The "Grunt Work" Growth Method

- Every time you face a task you think is beneath your skills, ask:
- *What skill is this teaching me?*
- *How can I make this process better for the next person?*
- Record 1 reflection at the end of each week.
- After 90 days, review: you'll see the hidden leadership lessons (patience, clarity, discipline).

APPLICATION: Turns "menial" work into leadership training instead of resentment.

3. CLARITY AND ACCOUNTABILITY

STORY CONNECTION: Leading small crews as a junior boatswain's mate.

TOOL: The Three-Part Instruction

PURPOSE: Deliver directions that eliminate confusion and prevent mistakes.

USE WHEN: You're assigning tasks, training people, or delegating work.

The Tool

1. What needs to be done

Clear, simple, observable.

2. Why it matters

Mission → relevance → consequence.

3. How success will be measured

- Define done. Define quality. Define timing.
- End by asking the team to repeat back the task in their own words.

APPLICATION: Prevents dangerous mistakes, builds accountability, and fosters trust.

4. SEIZING OPPORTUNITIES BEFORE THEY PASS

TOOL: The Opportunity Matrix (Modified Eisenhower Matrix)

Create a simple grid:

- **Aligned + Urgent** → Do now
- **Aligned + Not Urgent** → Prioritize (hidden gold)
- **Not Aligned + Urgent** → Delegate or decline
- **Not Aligned + Not Urgent** → Delete

HINT: If it's Aligned + Not Urgent, pursue it anyway. Don't wait until it's urgent—it may disappear.

APPLICATION: Protects leaders from the trap of short-sighted decisions they'll regret later.

5. CONSISTENCY IN MONOTONY

TOOL: The Consistency Compass

- Identify 3 daily non-negotiables (e.g., check ins with team, physical routine, personal reflection).
- Stick to them, especially in repetitive or stressful environments.
- Share them with your team so they see stability modeled.

APPLICATION: Provides a steady anchor when circumstances feel chaotic or draining.

6. EARLY LEADERSHIP RESET

TOOL: The Trust Equation (in practice)

- Trust = (Credibility + Reliability + Intimacy) ÷ Self-Orientation
- Ask yourself weekly:
  - *Am I credible? (Do I know my job?)*
  - *Am I reliable? (Do I follow through?)*
  - *Am I connected? (Do people feel safe with me?)*
  - *Am I self-oriented? (Am I making this about me instead of them?)*

APPLICATION: Keeps leaders grounded—evolves from proving themselves to empowering others.

KEY TAKEAWAYS

- Channel raw energy into productive action before it derails you.
- Menial work is often leadership training in disguise.
- Clarity and accountability keep teams safe and effective.
- Ignored opportunities become regrets—build a system to evaluate them.
- Leadership in monotony is about consistency, not charisma.
- Trust, not toughness, is the foundation of lasting leadership.
- Structure saved me—and it can save anyone willing to submit to it.

CHAPTER 4
STUCK IN THE MIDDLE

I ROSE THROUGH THE RANKS QUICKLY AT FIRST. BY THE end of my first enlistment, I had made E5. For a young sailor in the late 80s, that was quick—three years in, and I wore the second class crow. I thought that trajectory would keep going. I imagined E6 would come just as fast, then Chief, then maybe even Senior Chief. I had visions of stacking up rank like dominoes.

But then it stopped.

For ten long years, I stayed stuck at the same rank, like running on a treadmill while others sprinted past me on solid ground. Every exam season was the same cycle: study, test, wait, fail. Over time, I didn't even need to see the results—I could feel it in my gut before the scores came back.

By the time I found myself aboard my third ship, the USS Butte—an ammunition resupply vessel—I had about eight years in the Navy. On paper, I was seasoned. I had seen deployments, survived the grind of long underways, and built up a reputation for technical competence. But rank-wise, I was still a Second Class Petty Officer—squarely stuck in the middle.

That middle ground is tricky. You're not fresh anymore, so nobody cuts you slack. But you're not senior either, so you don't have authority to set the tone. You're expected to know your craft and execute it flawlessly, but you're also expected to keep your head down and not act like you know too much. I hadn't yet learned the art of balancing competence with humility, so I often stumbled onto the wrong side of that line.

I had made a promise to myself early on: I wasn't going to be one of those bitter sailors, always complaining about the system. My mantra became: *Get better, not bitter.* So I dove into my craft. I knew all my gear, cold. I studied manuals, practiced troubleshooting, and asked questions until I was confident I could outwork and outthink almost anyone in my rate.

That confidence was real—but it came with a shadow. To others, especially my Chief, it looked like arrogance. And honestly, he wasn't wrong. I thought I knew it all, and I carried myself that way. He didn't like me much, and the feeling was probably mutual.

THE INSPECTION

On the Butte, word came down that we were about to have a major inspection. In the Navy, inspections aren't just check-the-box exercises. They're career-making or career-breaking moments. Ships live and die by their readiness grades. A poor inspection could bring heat from higher command, while a great one could earn bragging rights, commendations, or even promotions.

Our Chief handed out assignments. Even though he didn't like me, he gave me responsibility: one section of our equipment to prepare and present. It was an important task, and I took it seriously.

When the inspection team arrived, the lead inspector turned out to be a senior officer who had once been enlisted in the same rate as me. In other words, he knew exactly what I knew—even more. That common ground created an instant connection.

When it was my turn, I walked him through my equipment. He listened closely, nodded, and asked sharp questions. I had the answers ready. He was impressed. But then something unexpected happened. Instead of moving on to the next sailor and the next station, he motioned for me to follow him. At the next system, he asked me for the rundown—even though someone else had been assigned to present it. I explained it anyway. At the next stop, he did the same thing. This went on all day.

By the time the inspection ended, I had essentially walked this senior officer through nearly the entire department's gear. I was proud. I had impressed a man who knew the trade inside out. And when it was over, he pulled my Chief aside and said something that, in hindsight, changed everything. He told him, "That sailor did an excellent job. You should be using him to train the rest of your staff."

I thought I had won. My Chief saw it differently.

THE CHEWING OUT

As soon as the inspectors left, my Chief lit into me. For thirty minutes, he tore me down. He told me I had embarrassed him and the division. He called me arrogant, self-serving, and a show-off. At the time, I thought it was jealousy. I thought, *He's just mad because the inspection officer liked me better.*

But years later, with perspective, I can admit he wasn't entirely wrong. That inspection carried three lessons I didn't see then but carry with me now.

Lesson One: Knowledge hoarded is just a secret.

I had mastered my craft, but I had kept it to myself. I could have shared what I knew with my shipmates before the inspection. I could have elevated the whole team. Instead, I hoarded it like a weapon, ready to show off when the moment came.

The truth is simple: knowledge that isn't shared doesn't strengthen the team. It just inflates the individual. And in any organization—whether it's a Navy division, a business, or a nonprofit—knowledge hoarding creates silos. Silos create resentment. And resentment kills trust.

TOOL FOR LEADERS: Ask yourself: Am I the only one who knows how this works? If the answer is Yes, you've created dependency. Real leadership equips others to succeed without you.

Lesson Two: It's not about the spotlight—it's about the team's win.

That day, I made the inspection about myself. Every answer I gave, every system I explained, reinforced the idea that I was the expert. What I didn't do was highlight my shipmates. I didn't affirm their work. I didn't share the stage.

A strong team doesn't thrive when one person dominates. It thrives when everyone contributes, when wins are shared, and when credit circulates freely. The individual spotlight may feel good, but it rarely builds cohesion.

TOOL FOR LEADERS: In moments of recognition, redirect praise. "Thank you—but it was my team who made this possible." That single sentence builds trust faster than any technical answer ever could.

Lesson Three: Leaders can unintentionally create imbalance.

The senior officer meant well. He saw talent and wanted to test it. But by pulling me through every station, he deprived other sailors of their chance to shine. Whether he realized it or not, he created the appearance of favoritism. And that perception poisoned the atmosphere.

Leaders must be careful with the spotlight. It's powerful. Too much focus on one person can alienate the rest of the team, even if the intent is good. Sometimes the most inclusive thing a leader can do is spread attention around.

TOOL FOR LEADERS: If you want to recognize talent, do it without stealing opportunity from others. Compliment the individual—but let everyone have their moment in front of you.

REFLECTION

That day on the Butte was humbling. In the moment, I thought I was being unfairly criticized. But time has taught me that my Chief, the inspector, and I all played a part in the lesson.

Leadership isn't about proving you know the most. It's about equipping others, spreading credit, and being intentional with how you use your influence. And, sometimes, the hardest lessons come wrapped in thirty minutes of words you don't want to hear.

THE WEIGHT OF MIDDLE RANK

Being an E5 meant I had authority, but not influence. I had responsibility, but not power. Sailors came to me for help, but officers looked right through me. I was in that awkward middle—too senior to hide in the shadows, too junior to have a seat at the real table.

It was frustrating. Demoralizing. And at times, humiliating.

When you're stuck in the middle long enough, you start to ask yourself dangerous questions: *Am I not good enough? Maybe this is all I'll ever be. Maybe leadership, real leadership, isn't for me.*

Those questions lived in my head for years.

And yet—this is where leadership forged me. Because

here's the truth: being stuck taught me more about leadership than any promotion ever did.

THE MENTORSHIP GAP

The Navy is built on mentorship, but mentorship is uneven. Some people fall into the hands of leaders who champion them, guide them, show them the ropes. Others—like me—float for years without that anchor.

I didn't have anyone pulling me aside to explain how advancement really worked. No one coached me on the boards, the politics, the subtleties beyond the written test. I was left to figure it out myself.

And I made mistakes. Plenty of them. I studied the wrong way. I treated leadership like authority instead of influence. I worked hard, but without direction. It felt like climbing a ladder where every third rung was missing. I could muscle my way up, but I scraped and bled for every inch.

CHIEF BUSH AND CHIEF ZICAFOOSE

My turning point came when two mentors appeared—Chief Bush and Chief Zicafoose.

Chief Bush was the kind of leader you never forget. He didn't just tell you what to do—he invested in you. He pulled me aside one day and said, "White, you've got the potential, but potential without preparation is wasted." He fought to get me into technical schools that I had been passed over for in the past. Those schools gave me the deeper knowledge I had been missing, the kind that separated competent sailors from experts.

Then came Chief Zicafoose. If Bush gave me the technical foundation, she gave me the administrative and academic edge. She was precise, sharp, and relentless. She taught me how to handle the paperwork, the systems, the details behind the job. More importantly, she taught me how to study.

Before her, I would just brute-force my way through exam prep—reading, rereading, hoping something would stick. Under her guidance, I learned strategy. She broke down the exam for me, taught me how to study by topic weight, how to dissect questions, and how to master the advancement system instead of letting it master me. The result? I scored in the top 99th percentile of all test takers in my rate.

And yet, even that wasn't enough.

WHEN EXCELLENCE STILL WASN'T ENOUGH

I'll never forget the moment I saw my test results. Top 99th percentile. On paper, I was one of the best in the country in my rate. For the first time in a long time, I felt like I had undeniable proof that I belonged at the next level.

But the Navy doesn't work on proof alone. Advancement also depends on quotas—how many billets are open at the next pay grade. And that year, the quota for my rate at E6 was microscopic. No matter how well I scored, the math was against me.

I can still feel the sting of that letdown. It was like being told, "You're ready, but we don't need you yet."

It would have been easy to give up, to sink back into bitterness and blame the system. But this is where the power of mentorship showed its true force.

CHIEF ZICAFOOSE'S ADVOCACY

Chief Zicafoose refused to let me stall again. She didn't just teach me to study—she fought for me.

She pulled my record, highlighted my evaluations, documented the impact of the sailors I had led, and built a case that my performance spoke louder than any quota chart. Then she did something I'll never forget—she lobbied for me to be advanced through a performance-based program.

This program was about demonstrated leadership, job performance, and impact. She stood in front of senior leaders and put her credibility on the line for me.

And it worked.

When the message came down that I was being advanced to E6, it wasn't just a promotion. It was validation. Not just of my ability, but of the belief that sometimes all someone needs is for a leader to step into the gap on their behalf.

FROM FRUSTRATION TO FUEL

When you've been stuck as long as I had, something changes inside you. You stop obsessing over the next stripe on your sleeve and start asking: *What kind of leader am I becoming right now?*

I realized that I had two choices: let bitterness harden me, or let frustration sharpen me. I chose sharpening. The sailors who looked up to me—whether the Navy promoted me or not—were watching how I handled being overlooked. And I refused to let them see a leader who gave up.

I started showing up differently. Instead of grumbling about my stalled career, I poured my energy into theirs.

STORIES OF MENTORSHIP

There was one young sailor—I'll call him Ramirez—who reminded me of myself in my early days. Hardworking, but rough around the edges. He didn't think he had a chance at advancement. I pulled him aside one night after watch and said, "Ramirez, you're not going to fail on my watch. If I know something, you're going to know it. If I can do something, you'll learn how to do it too."

We studied together. I showed him how to break down the advancement manual the way Chief Zicafoose had shown me. When the results came out, he pinned on his next rank. I'll never forget the look on his face when he realized he had done it. That moment hit me harder than any of my own promotions—because I knew I had passed on the gift that was given to me.

Another sailor, Thomas, had been written off by other leaders as a troublemaker. Instead of sending him to mast, I gave him responsibility—real responsibility. I told him, "If you want to prove everyone wrong, start here." He rose to the challenge, and later became one of my most reliable petty officers. That was when I learned another leadership truth: sometimes, giving responsibility is the best form of discipline.

LEARNING TO LEAD WITHOUT THE RANK

The more I invested in others, the less the sting of my stalled rank bothered me. Slowly, my measure of leadership shifted from the stripes on my uniform to the growth of the people under my charge.

It was liberating. For the first time, I stopped chasing advancement for its own sake and started building a reputation for impact. And ironically—that shift was what made me undeniable when my mentors pushed for me to advance.

THE BREAKTHROUGH TO E6

When I finally pinned on E6 through the performance-based program, I didn't see it as my victory alone. I saw it as the fruit of mentorship. Chief Bush, Chief Zicafoose, and the sailors I had poured into—they all had fingerprints on that promotion.

It was the slowest promotion of my career, but the most important. It wasn't just about climbing another rung on the ladder—it was about proving that mentorship, perseverance, and advocacy could overcome even the cold math of quotas.

MINDSET SHIFTS THAT LASTED

That season of stagnation gave me convictions that I carried through the rest of my Navy career and into my civilian leadership:

- Promotions can be delayed, but growth never should be. Even when the system stalls you, you can keep learning, improving, and leading.
- Mentorship isn't optional—it's oxygen. Leaders who hoard knowledge choke the growth of others.
- Leadership is stewardship. You don't own your position—you hold it for the sake of those you serve.
- Impact precedes title. You don't become a leader because

of a promotion; you earn promotion because of your leadership.

CLOSING REFLECTION: LEADERSHIP IN THE MIDDLE

Looking back, those ten years in the "middle" taught me something I never would've learned if I'd been promoted quickly: true leadership is forged in frustration.

It's easy to lead when recognition is pouring in and promotions stack up. It's harder to lead when you're overlooked, when the system says no, when you start to doubt yourself. That's when character is tested.

And here's the lesson I carry with me to this day: being stuck is not the end—it's the classroom where resilience, humility, and mentorship are taught.

Because of that decade, I don't just value rank—I value the people who build you, and the people you build. Without Bush, without Zicafoose, without the sailors I mentored along the way, I would've just been another frustrated E5. Instead, I became the kind of leader who knows that advancement is not just about what you achieve—it's about who you bring with you.

Being "stuck in the middle" isn't failure—it's formation. Leadership is often forged in the grind of waiting, mentoring, and proving that impact is bigger than rank.

FRAMEWORK: FOUR ANCHORS OF MIDDLE LEADERSHIP

1. **Growth Without Promotion:** Advancement may stall, but learning and influence must continue.

2. **Mentorship as Oxygen:** Leaders thrive when they both receive and give guidance.
3. **Impact Before Title:** Influence comes from serving others, not from stripes or titles.
4. **Stewardship of the Role:** Your position isn't owned—it's held for the sake of those you serve.

TOOL: The Middle-Map

USE WHEN: You feel stuck or overlooked, use this map to reframe your leadership:

Step 1: Audit Your Growth

- *What skills or knowledge am I building even if my title hasn't changed?*
- *Where am I sharper today than I was a year ago?*

Step 2: Identify Mentorship Gaps

- *Who is pouring into me right now?*
- *Who am I intentionally pouring into?*

Step 3: Expand Impact Without Authority

- *What responsibilities can I take on that demonstrate readiness beyond my rank?*
- *How can I lead through influence instead of position?*

Step 4: Advocate With Evidence

- *What proof of my leadership impact (projects, people, results) can I prepare now, so others can advocate for me later?*

Reflection: Check Yourself

- Do I measure my leadership by rank, or by the growth of others?
- Am I letting bitterness stall me, or am I letting frustration sharpen me?
- Who around me could rise if I invested in them the way I wish someone had invested in me?

Exercise: The Mentorship Chain

- **Upstream:** Write down one person you can approach to mentor you in the next 30 days.
- **Downstream:** Write down one person you will mentor, coach, or invest in over the next 30 days.
- **Action:** Schedule both conversations this week.

Closing Anchor

Leadership in the middle isn't about waiting for recognition—it's about proving that growth, mentorship, and impact matter more than the pace of promotion.

CHAPTER 4 PLAYBOOK
LEADING FROM THE MIDDLE

1. REFRAME THE WAITING SEASON

TOOL: The Growth Grid

- **Step 1:** List 3 skills you can grow regardless of promotion (technical, communication, leadership).
- **Step 2:** Break each skill into a 90-day learning sprint with 1 measurable outcome.
- **Step 3:** Share progress with a peer or mentor for accountability.
- **Step 4:** Reassess every 6 months—track growth, not just promotions.

APPLICATION: Keeps motivation alive even when recognition has stalled.

2. FIND OR BUILD MENTORSHIP

TOOL: The Mentorship Map

- **Step 1:** Identify gaps (technical, administrative, leadership, networking).
- **Step 2:** List 2–3 people who excel in each area.
- **Step 3:** Approach them with one specific ask (e.g., "Can you show me how you prepare for boards?").
- **Step 4:** Track lessons learned in a "Mentorship Journal."

APPLICATION: Ensures you don't wait passively for mentorship—you curate it.

3. LEAD WITHOUT THE TITLE

TOOL: The 3×3 Mentorship Rule

- Choose 3 juniors to intentionally invest in.
- Meet 3 times a month (formal or informal).
- Cover 3 areas: technical growth, personal accountability, and career advancement.
- Celebrate their wins publicly, document their progress privately.

APPLICATION: Builds legacy and influence even before official recognition.

4. ADVOCACY AS LEADERSHIP

TOOL: The Advocacy Packet
For yourself or others:

1. Gather performance metrics (achievements, impact).
2. Collect endorsements (quotes, eval bullets).
3. Highlight the growth of those you've mentored.
4. Package into a one-page "impact brief" for supervisors.

APPLICATION: Equips leaders to make themselves—and their people—visible when systems overlook them.

5. SHIFT FROM RANK TO IMPACT

TOOL: Weekly Reflection Prompt
Ask yourself every Friday:

- Who did I grow this week?
- What system/process did I leave better than I found it?
- If I left tomorrow, what would my legacy be?

APPLICATION: Keeps focus on leadership influence, not just personal advancement.

KEY TAKEAWAYS

- Growth doesn't pause for quotas. Even if the system stalls, personal development doesn't.
- Mentorship changes the game. Seek it, give it, and advocate for others.

- Leadership without rank is possible. Influence is built in the everyday, not just in titles.
- Advocacy is part of leadership. Fight for others as hard as you wish someone would fight for you.
- Bitter or Better—your choice. Seasons of waiting forge either cynicism or resilience.

CHAPTER 5

THE MAKING OF A CHIEF

BY THE TIME I PINNED ON E6, I FELT SOMETHING inside me shift. After years of being stuck at E5—fighting the system, fighting myself, and fighting to be recognized—I finally had momentum. And with that momentum came new opportunities, new mentors, and eventually, a new level of responsibility that would transform me into the leader I was meant to become.

I transferred to the Navy Cargo Handling Battalion, a unit responsible for the logistics of loading and offloading the massive prepositioning ships that carried everything a Marine battalion would need to land and sustain itself—hospital units, tanks, water purification, tents, even toilet paper. The work was demanding, technical, and dangerous. It was also where I began to understand the power of recognition.

Shortly after my first year, I was named Sailor of the Year for my command. Under the mentorship of Senior Chief Grimm, I not only competed but advanced through two higher levels of competition. I didn't win the whole thing, but the process itself was transformative. It forced me to sharpen my communication skills and refine my professional presence, and allowed me to believe that I had something to offer beyond brute effort.

Senior Chief Grimm showed me what it looked like to advocate for someone, to push them into the spotlight—not because they were ready, but because it was time to stretch. His mentorship reinforced what I had learned from Bush and Zicafoose: leaders see in you what you don't see in yourself, and they push you to rise. And they provide a "soft landing" if things don't go as planned.

INTO THE ICE: ANTARCTICA

At Cargo Handling, I was introduced to missions few sailors ever experience and one of the most memorable deployments of my career: Antarctica. The mission was straightforward on paper: offload the supply vessel at the Arctic research facility at McMurdo Station, and take back retrograde cargo. In reality, it was grueling. The weather was brutal. The equipment froze. Every movement required precision and endurance.

The first year, I went as part of the team. The second year, I led my own crew. Standing on the ice, coordinating the offload of massive containers in near-zero visibility, I realized something important: leadership doesn't always look like a speech or a strategy. Sometimes, it looks like standing in the cold with your people, making the same sacrifices, showing them that the standard applies to everyone—including you.

That mission taught me resilience, but more than that, it taught me visibility. Leaders can't just be present in words or memos. They have to be physically there when the work is hardest.

THE ROAD TO CHIEF

My time at Cargo Handling was also where I got my first taste of combat-style training. Until then, my career had been largely shipboard. But here, expeditionary readiness was part of the culture. Weapons training, security drills, small-unit tactics—skills I had only brushed against before now became part of my toolkit.

It was at this command, under pressure and challenge, that my peers and seniors began to see me differently. Not just as a hard worker or a fighter, but as someone ready for the next level.

And then it happened: I was selected for Chief Petty Officer.

Becoming a Chief in the Navy (advancing from E6 to E7) is unlike any other promotion. It isn't just about rank—it's about identity. You put on khakis for the first time, joining a tradition that stretches back more than a century. You become part of the Chief's Mess, a brotherhood and sisterhood of leaders expected to set the tone for the entire enlisted force.

But the transition isn't automatic. At the time I was promoted, it was still called "initiation"—a grueling, humbling, and transformative process designed to strip away ego and rebuild you as the kind of leader who could carry the weight of the anchors you now wore. It wasn't about hazing or humiliation. It was about building resilience, humility, and connection. It was about making you understand that, from this point forward, you didn't belong to yourself—you belonged to your sailors.

THE CAPTAIN'S TEST

When I first arrived at my next ship, the USS Anzio, I walked into a division that had been without a first class (E6) for months. Discipline was loose. Standards were slipping. Training was inconsistent. I got to work immediately, instilling structure, setting expectations, and getting my sailors qualified. Within months, the division was running like clockwork.

At first, the Captain praised me. He was relieved to finally have someone to take charge and run the division. But after I put on khakis (made Chief), his attitude shifted. The things that had impressed him as an E6 were now considered baseline. The bar had been raised.

My first set of evaluations as a Chief? I was ranked dead last—30 of 30. It was a gut punch. I could have given up, complained, or coasted. Instead, I doubled down. I poured myself into developing my sailors, pushing them to qualify, to study, to advance. For two cycles in a row, my sailors had a 100 percent advancement rate. Every single one who took the test moved up.

By the time I left that ship, I had gone from last to first. I was ranked number one of 30.

The lesson was etched deep: what gets you here won't keep you here. Past performance is just the entry ticket. Once you step into a new level of leadership, the expectations rise. You don't get to rest on yesterday's accomplishments.

THE CALL OF THE EXPEDITIONARY

Then came September 11, 2001. The world changed, and so did the Navy. In response, the Navy created new expeditionary combat units—mobile, agile, and focused on force protection and anti-terrorism.

I volunteered immediately.

At first, I was sent to California for advanced weapons and small-boat tactical training, learning from Navy Special Warfare Combatant-Craft Crewmen (SWCC). We learned to interdict; to deter; to defend; and to maneuver those fast, armored boats through high-threat environments.

From there, I was sent to Guam to help stand up a brand-new unit: Mobile Security Squadron 7. I was responsible for the waterside element—five boats, twenty-seven sailors, and a mission to protect high-value assets and deter terrorist threats.

Training those sailors from scratch, watching them evolve from novices to highly skilled operators, was one of the most rewarding experiences of my career. We worked hard. We trained harder. And when the mission came—night operations off the coast of the Philippines, deterring terrorists moving by boat—we were ready.

The unit performed at a level that exceeded every standard. And for me, it cemented something I had been building all along: the best teams aren't built by chance. They're built by leaders who set high expectations, invest in training, and create a culture where excellence is the norm.

The anchors of a Chief had reshaped me. The deployments, the teams, the victories, and the challenges forged me into a Senior Chief. I believed I had finally caught the rhythm of a career that could go the full thirty years. For the first time in a long time, I felt like the Navy and I were in step.

But there's a saying in uniform: "The Navy always gets a vote".

SIXTY SECONDS IN THE SUEZ

The Suez Canal is one of those places you can't fully appreciate until you've been there. On a map, it looks like a simple line carved through the desert of Egypt, but when you're on the water, the magnitude hits you. A hundred and twenty miles of narrow waterway, bordered by dry sand, watchtowers, villages, and, at times, nothing but endless horizon. Billions of dollars of cargo move through it every single day, making it one of the most strategically important places in the world.

By the time I found myself steaming through those waters with a small team of armed sailors under my command, I had deployed multiple times and made enough mistakes to know leadership wasn't about perfection—it was about persistence and responsibility.

Still, the Suez was different. The pace was slow, the canal banks were close, and threats could materialize in seconds.

Our mission was straightforward: provide security for a massive merchant ship carrying cargo through the canal. The Navy had realized that these ships were juicy targets on the open ocean, so we embedded security detachments, like mine, to keep watch. That meant standing on deck, weapons ready, radios on, eyes scanning every ripple in the water and every shadow on shore.

Most of the time, it was mind-numbingly routine. Twelve-hour watches. Heat that soaked through your body. Endlessly scanning the same desert shoreline. Still, we took the job seriously because we knew complacency was the enemy. The one time you relax is the time something happens.

That morning, the ship was crawling forward at about twelve miles an hour. The sun was already beating down, bouncing off the sand and water, turning everything into a blinding reflection. We had an Egyptian liaison officer on board—a requirement of the canal—polite but distant. He had one job: observe and report to his superiors.

I remember thinking how normal it all felt. I grabbed a cup of coffee and made my way toward the pilot house. Just another transit. Just another day. That's the trap of leadership—right when you convince yourself things are predictable, life throws you a curveball.

Halfway through my coffee, it hit.

Pop! Pop-pop-pop!

Gunfire.

At first, I thought my ears were playing tricks. But then came more—five, six, maybe eight sharp cracks in rapid succession. The kind of sound you don't mistake once you've been around weapons as long as I had.

My heart rate spiked instantly. Training took over. I sprinted up to the pilot house, coffee forgotten, ears tuned for the chaos I knew was about to unfold.

By the time I got there, my radio was already alive with chatter. "Shots fired, shots fired! Starboard side!"

My gunners were scanning, weapons trained, adrenaline pouring into every word they said.

One voice came through clear: "Target acquired. Weapons release?"

Weapons release. That was on me. I had the authority. It meant one of my gunners had a potential hostile in his sights, and all it would take was one word from me—"fire"—and rounds would be flying.

I turned to the Egyptian liaison officer, who was standing stiff in the pilot house. "Did you hear that?" I demanded.

His face was calm, almost too calm. He shook his head. "I heard nothing."

That answer didn't sit right. I turned back to the radio.

"Target acquired, weapons release!" another voice called out. This wasn't training anymore. My team wasn't asking for fun. They were ready to unleash lethal force, and they were waiting on me.

And in that moment, time slowed down. Leadership will do that to you.

Inside my head, a thousand thoughts raced. Who was shooting? Pirates? Terrorists? Or was it something else? If I gave the order and my team fired on the wrong people—say, Egyptian military escorts—that decision could ignite an international crisis. On the flip side, if I hesitated and the threat was real, my indecision could cost lives.

Sixty seconds. That's all I had.

"Check fire, check fire!" one of my gunners called, his voice cutting through the static. Essentially: hold your fire and evaluate what's going on. Then another update: "They're jumping! They're abandoning the vehicle!"

And just like that, the pieces fell into place. On either side of the canal, Egyptian jeeps had been shadowing us, mounted with machine guns. They were supposed to be protecting us. But one of those gunners had accidentally fired. My team, trained and alert, reacted instantly. But when the Egyptians saw us swing our weapons toward them, panic set in. They bailed out of their own jeeps, afraid we'd unleash hell in return.

I exhaled slowly, tension draining from my body. Crisis averted. We didn't fire. No one died. And yet, I knew something important had just been etched into my DNA.

Leadership under pressure isn't about having all the answers. It's about staying calm enough to collect the facts, trusting your training, and making the best decision you can with the information you have—knowing full well that consequences follow either way.

That moment in the Suez taught me that sometimes the best leadership decision is restraint. Not firing can be just as powerful as firing—if you're confident in your judgment, your team will trust you enough to hold fire when every instinct screams otherwise.

THE END OF ONE CHAPTER

I had checked every box, earned every award, had stellar evaluations, led teams through the kind of missions most sailors only hear about in stories. I was convinced that Master Chief was just a matter of time. My evals were strong, my sailors were excelling, my record was stacked with deployments and impact. I bet everything on it.

And then the list came out. My name wasn't there.

The disappointment hit harder than any fistfight, harder than any rejection I had ever known. Because this wasn't just about rank—it was about identity. For 26 years, I had been a sailor. A leader. A Chief. And then a Senior Chief. Surely, I would make Master Chief.

And suddenly, the clock ran out. High Year Tenure meant I couldn't wait another cycle. My career ended, not with a retirement ceremony planned years in advance, but with a blunt deadline: you're done. I didn't make Master Chief.

I had spent my life leading men and women across oceans, through storms, into missions where failure wasn't an option. But now I stood on the pier with no uniform, no mission, no plan. For the first time since I was 17 years old, I wasn't in the Navy. And I had no idea what came next.

I told you, the Navy always gets a vote.

KEY LEADERSHIP LESSONS FROM MAKING CHIEF

- Mentorship is oxygen. You can't rise without people who believe in you and open doors you can't open yourself.
- Recognition is fuel. Sailor of the Year didn't make me a better leader, but the process of competing did—it forced me to grow.
- Visibility matters. Your people need to see you in the trenches, not just hear from you.
- Expectations rise with rank. What impressed others as an E6 was mediocre as a Chief. Leadership is about constant growth.
- Teams don't form—they're forged. Training, trust, and shared sacrifice turn a group of individuals into a unit.
- Sometimes the best leadership decision is restraint.

This chapter of my life was about transformation—stepping into the anchors of a Chief, learning to lead not just by example but by expectation, and embracing the truth that leadership is not about the authority you wear, but the standard you embody.

THE FOUR ANCHORS OF CHIEF LEADERSHIP

1. Visibility in the Trenches

- Leaders show up physically when the work is hardest
- Presence communicates shared sacrifice and shared standards
- Your people need to see you, not just hear from you

Framework: The Visibility Check

- Weekly: *Where is my team struggling most?*
- Monthly: *When did I last work alongside (not just observe) my people?*
- Quarterly: *What hard work am I avoiding that I'm asking others to do?*

2. Expectations Rise with Rank

- What got you promoted becomes the new baseline
- Past performance is the entry ticket, not the permanent pass
- Each level demands growth, not repetition

Framework: The Reset Practice

- At every promotion/transition, identify what worked before that won't work now
- Identify 2-3 new skills you must develop at this level
- Ask a trusted peer: "What looks impressive at my old level, but is average at this one?"

3. Crisis Demands Clarity

- In high-pressure moments, information becomes currency
- Train your team to bring options, not just problems
- Create a culture where people can pivot without ego

Framework: The 60-Second Decision Process

- **Pause & Scan:** Expect change, take one breath to reset
- **Collect & Filter:** Demand facts and options from your team
- **Decide & Adjust:** Act fast, but leave room for course corrections

4. Teams Are Forged, Not Formed

- Excellence is built through shared challenge and shared success
- Investment in people creates exponential returns
- The best teams are those you develop, not those you inherit

Framework: The Team Forge Cycle

- **Train:** Build skills until they become second nature
- **Trust:** Give your team real responsibility, even if they stumble
- **Test:** Create controlled challenges that stretch your team's capabilities

Quick Reference: Leading Under Pressure

USE WHEN: The stakes are highest:

- Be where your people can see you
- Raise your standards, don't lower them
- Demand clarity from your team
- Invest in their growth, not just the mission

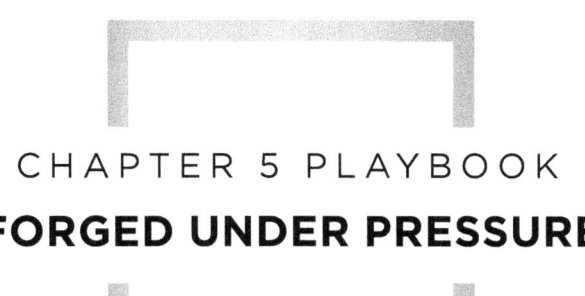

CHAPTER 5 PLAYBOOK
FORGED UNDER PRESSURE

1. MENTORSHIP MAP

TOOL: Create a "Mentorship Map" with three circles:

- Above you: Who is guiding you (mentors)?
- Beside you: Who is challenging you (peers)?
- Below you: Who is learning from you (mentees)?

ACTION STEP: Write one concrete action this week for each circle (e.g., schedule a mentor call, share feedback with a peer, or intentionally coach someone junior).

2. VISIBILITY AUDIT

TOOL: List your team's toughest, least glamorous tasks.

ACTION STEP: Commit to showing up physically at one of these moments this month (e.g., stay late with your team on a deadline, pull a shift in the field, walk the floor during high-stress periods).

Purpose: Presence in the trenches builds credibility faster than speeches do.

3. RAISING THE BAR FRAMEWORK

When promoted or stepping into a bigger role:

1. **Define Baseline:** Write down what you did that got you promoted.
2. **Set New Standards:** Identify 2-3 ways you must grow to succeed at the next level (e.g., delegation, communication, strategy).
3. **Feedback Check:** Ask a trusted peer or mentor, "What looks good at my old level, but is average at this one?"

4. RECOGNITION RITUALS

TOOL: Build a recognition practice into your leadership routine.

ACTION STEP:
- **Daily:** Say Thank You for small wins in the moment.
- **Weekly:** Highlight one person's contribution in front of the team.
- **Quarterly:** Nominate someone for formal recognition (awards, promotions, or external programs).

PURPOSE: Recognition is fuel. Done consistently, it drives growth and retention.

5. FORGING A TEAM UNDER PRESSURE

TOOL: Use the "Train-Trust-Test" cycle.

1. Train your team in skills and standards until it's second nature.
2. Trust them with real responsibility, even if they stumble.
3. Test them with controlled challenges (simulations, stress drills, stretch assignments).

ACTION STEP: Identify one area where you can "Train-Trust-Test" your people this quarter.

Reflection Questions

- Where am I visible to my team during their hardest work?
- What expectations do I need to raise for this new level of leadership?
- How do I handle incomplete information under pressure?
- Who on my team is ready for more responsibility than I'm giving them?
- Who are my mentors right now, and am I letting them push me into the spotlight?
- Am I still operating at the level I was promoted from—or at the level I've been promoted to?
- How often do I intentionally recognize and celebrate my people?
- What am I doing to forge—not just form—a high-performing team?

Key Takeaways

- The Chief's anchors aren't about the uniform—they're about the weight of responsibility and the clarity of purpose that comes when people depend on you to lead them.
- What gets you here won't keep you here. Each level of leadership demands reinvention.
- Visibility in the hardest moments builds a credibility that lasts.
- The best teams are forged through intentional training, trust, and testing.
- Sometimes, the most powerful decision is restraint—knowing when not to act is as important as knowing when to act.

CHAPTER 6
REINVENTION AND REDISCOVERY

I WALKED OFF THE BASE FOR THE LAST TIME WITH NO orders in my hand. For 26 years, the Navy had told me where to go, what to do, and who I was. Now, for the first time since I was 17, nobody was waiting on the other side. No uniform, no mission, no plan. Just silence.

The truth is—I wasn't ready. Not financially, not emotionally, not even mentally. The Navy had offered countless opportunities to get a degree, to prepare for transition, to line up certifications. But I had convinced myself I didn't need them. I was going to make thirty years, retire, and never have to work again. That was the plan.

But the plan died the day I missed Master Chief. And truth be told, it was never a good plan to begin with.

I had believed the stories, too—the ones passed around every command: "When you get out, companies will line up to pay you six figures. You've got discipline, a clean haircut, no drug habits, and leadership experience. You'll be set." I clung to that belief, because the alternative was admitting I had no idea how to survive outside the gates.

And then reality hit.

THE SURVIVAL SEASON

With less than a month to my actual retirement, I had to face the truth. My pension would be less than fifty percent of my paycheck. The housing allowance, the benefits, the entitlements—all gone. And I didn't have a job lined up. After decades of structure and planning every mission down to the smallest detail, I had no plan for the biggest mission of all: my own future.

Desperation forced me to make a quick decision. I accepted a job at a distribution center in Philadelphia, six hours away from my home in Virginia. For two years, I worked brutal twelve-hour weekend shifts, driving six hours each way. I was hired as a "high potential" candidate and eventually rotated through management, learning to lead teams of thirty without the authority of rank. These weren't sailors—they were people working for a paycheck who could quit anytime. I had to learn influence without authority, fast.

The warehouse taught me humility and introduced me to process improvement methodologies like Lean and Six Sigma principles, but the cost was devastating. I missed family dinners, kids' activities, and time at home. My wife, who had carried the weight of military life through my deployments, was now carrying the weight of my absence all over again—even though I was technically "home."

After two years, she gave me the ultimatum I knew was

coming: come home for good, or keep losing the family I had sacrificed so much for.

I chose home. I took a pay cut and returned to Virginia.

Financially, it didn't make much difference—the gas and wear-and-tear had eaten most of my paycheck—but personally, it was everything.

BACK TO SCHOOL, BACK TO MYSELF

Once I was back in Virginia, I had a moment of clarity: I didn't want to work with my body anymore. Years of military service had taken a toll. The warehouse grind had proved it. I needed to use my mind.

So I went back to school and earned my degree in business. Along the way, I stumbled onto something that would change the entire trajectory of my life: project management.

At first, I didn't understand it. But as I dug deeper, I realized project management was simply a name for what I had been doing my entire military career—leading teams, organizing complex missions, balancing time, cost, and performance. For the first time since retirement, I felt a spark of recognition.

I began preparing for the PMP certification—the gold standard in project management. One night, while researching, I discovered that Hampton Roads had a local PMI (Project Management Institute) chapter. They were hosting an event that Wednesday. I bought a ticket.

Walking into that room was intimidating. These were polished professionals, speaking a language I didn't fully know yet. Acronyms, methodologies, certifications—it felt like stepping into a different world with a new language. But something inside me clicked. These were my people.

I even tried to volunteer that same night, despite not being a member yet. They told me to slow down, but it didn't matter. I knew I had found the place where I could rebuild my professional identity.

FINDING MY PEOPLE IN PMI

Over the next seven years, I threw myself into PMI. I started as Military Liaison Director, helping transitioning service members see the connection between their skills and project management. Then I became VP of Membership, bringing in new professionals and growing the chapter. From there, VP of Operations—managing logistics for events, conferences, and networking nights. Eventually, I rose to President of the 1,500-member chapter.

Each role taught me something new. Unlike the Navy, I had no rank to lean on. These were volunteers, not subordinates. They didn't have to show up. They didn't have to listen. If they felt unappreciated, they could walk away.

That meant I had to lead differently. I had to lead through passion, vision, and persuasion. I had to inspire people to give their time and energy freely. And that, I discovered, is the purest form of influence: authority without rank.

Each PMI role taught me civilian leadership. As Military Liaison Director, I translated military experience into business language. As VP of Operations, I managed logistics without command structure. As President, I cast vision and drove results while maintaining the volunteer spirit.

THE ART OF VOLUNTEER LEADERSHIP

Leading volunteers taught me things the military never could. In the Navy, people showed up because they had to. Orders were orders. In PMI, people showed up because they wanted to. That changed everything.

I had to master the art of influence without authority. Instead of giving orders, I had to paint pictures. Instead of demanding compliance, I had to earn commitment. Instead of relying on rank, I had to rely on relationships.

REDISCOVERING PURPOSE

Through PMI, I also rediscovered something that had been dormant since leaving the Navy: a sense of mission larger than myself. In the military, that mission was clear—defend the country, protect your shipmates, complete the objective. In civilian life, purpose felt muddier.

But after watching transitioning veterans struggle with the same identity crisis I had faced, I found my new mission: helping others navigate the gap between who they were and who they could become. Whether it was teaching project management principles, mentoring new professionals, or simply showing up consistently for people who needed guidance—and not just military guidance.

At every level of the corporate space as well, I was serving again.

The skills were transferable, but the application was completely different. Instead of leading sailors through dangerous waters, I was leading professionals through career transitions. Instead of managing military logistics, I was managing volunteer organizations. Instead of following orders, I was creating vision.

FAMILY, BALANCE, AND GROWTH

None of this would have been possible without my wife's support. At one point, I was working full-time, going to school full-time, studying for the PMP, and volunteering for PMI. For two years, I practically disappeared into my room every night—I was either reading, writing, or attending networking events. My family carried me through it, even when they were frustrated or tired of my absence.

But this time, the absence felt different. In Philadelphia, I was working to survive. Now I was working to build something. The family could see the purpose, even when the pace was exhausting.

My wife would often joke that she had "lost [me] to PMI," but she said it with pride, not resentment. She could see that I was becoming myself again—not the struggling veteran trying to find his way, but the leader who had something to offer.

THE TRANSFORMATION

By the time I finished my tenure as PMI President, I was a different person than the one who had walked off the base seven years earlier. I had discovered that leadership principles are universal, but their application is infinite. I had learned that influence without authority is actually more powerful than authority without influence. And I had proven to myself that reinvention isn't just possible—it's essential.

This was my proving ground. The Navy had shaped me. The warehouse had humbled me. School had equipped me. But PMI—and the world of project management—rebuilt me. And through it all, I had discovered that the end of one career doesn't have to mean the end of purpose—it can mean the beginning of a new way to serve.

KEY LEADERSHIP LESSONS FROM REINVENTION

- Transition is identity shock. You don't just leave a career—you leave a community, a rhythm, and an identity. Plan for it.
- Family anchors matter more than titles. Choosing home over a paycheck saved my marriage and my sanity.
- Volunteer leadership is a true test. When people can walk away, the only thing that keeps them is your ability to inspire.
- Reinvention requires humility. Being willing to start over, to be the beginner again, is the price of growth.
- Skills without a name are invisible. I had been doing project management for decades, but until I called it that, no one saw it.
- Influence without authority is the purest form of leadership. When you can't rely on rank, you must rely on relationships, vision, and service.
- Purpose can be rediscovered. The mission doesn't end—it transforms.

This chapter of my life was about rediscovery—of who I was outside the Navy, of what leadership meant without rank, and of the fact that reinvention isn't a one-time event. It's a lifelong discipline.

CHAPTER 6 PLAYBOOK
REINVENTION AND REDISCOVERY

FRAMEWORK: THE REINVENTION MAP

Reinvention moves in phases. Every major transition—personal, professional, spiritual, or identity-based—follows a predictable emotional and strategic arc.

USE THIS MAP: To understand where you are and what each phase requires.

PHASE 1: DISRUPTION AND GROUNDING (MONTHS 1–6)

Reality: Something changes—an ending, a shift, or an unexpected opportunity. Your internal and external world feels unstable, and you're under pressure to "figure things out" quickly.

ACTION: Focus on immediate stability: routines, financial grounding, emotional regulation, and short-term decisions that keep you moving without locking you into a permanent direction.

MINDSET: This is a grounding season. You don't need answers yet—just space, clarity, and steady steps.

PHASE 2: EXPLORATION AND IDENTITY REBUILDING (MONTHS 6–12)

REALITY: The initial shock fades, and you begin to rediscover who you are without the old labels, roles, or expectations. Curiosity increases. Old interests fade; new ones emerge.

ACTION: Experiment. Try things with low commitment—projects, roles, communities, learning opportunities, creative pursuits. Collect data about what energizes you, challenges you, or feels aligned.

MINDSET: Treat this phase like a laboratory. You're not choosing a path yet—you're exploring possibilities.

PHASE 3: ALIGNMENT AND DIRECTION SETTING (YEAR 1–2)

REALITY: Clarity begins to take shape. Patterns emerge. You start recognizing what feels right, what drains you, and what your next chapter might demand.

ACTION: Begin shaping a direction: define priorities, set initial goals, identify what you will and won't accept moving forward. Build systems and boundaries that reflect your evolving identity.

MINDSET: You're transitioning from exploration to intention. Don't rush it—alignment is more important than speed.

PHASE 4: CONSTRUCTION AND CAPABILITY BUILDING (YEAR 2-3)

REALITY: You've chosen a direction and now need skills, structure, and support to build the life or career you're aiming for.

ACTION: Invest in development—training, coaching, certifications, strengthening your network, deepening mastery. Build habits and systems that sustain growth.

MINDSET: This is the foundation phase. What you build here determines the stability and scale of your next chapter.

PHASE 5: INTEGRATION AND EXPANSION (YEAR 3+)

REALITY: Your new identity, direction, or purpose becomes your norm. You move with increased confidence and clarity.

ACTION: Expand—take on leadership roles, pursue advanced goals, scale your impact, refine your craft. Support others going through similar transitions.

MINDSET: Reinvention becomes integration. You're not the person who entered Phase 1—and that's the point.

CLOSING PERSPECTIVE

Reinvention is cyclical. You'll move through these phases more than once in your lifetime. But each time you do, you'll have more clarity, more resilience, and a stronger foundation to navigate the next transition with purpose.

TOOL: Family Anchor Check-In
Transition doesn't happen in a vacuum. Your family carries the weight of uncertainty, too.

ANCHOR CONVERSATIONS:
- Schedule a monthly family sit-down to discuss:
  - What's working?
  - What's draining us?
  - What do we need to adjust?
- Use a 1–10 scale for areas like time together, financial stability, and stress level

ACTION: Pick one adjustment to make each month based on the scores.

TOOL: Influence Without Authority Playbook
Leadership outside the military (or any structured system) requires a shift from authority to influence.

1. **Profile the Work**: Break down the task into clear, measurable outcomes

2. **Profile the People**: Identify the strengths, skills, and motivation levels of your team
3. **Pair the Two**: Match the right person to the right task for maximum ownership. Write down how you matched people to tasks
4. **Lead by Presence**: Be visible in the work, not just in the results

ACTION: Next time you lead a project, review what worked and what didn't.

TOOL: Process Improvement Mindset
The introduction to Lean and Six Sigma showed me leadership is also about systems.

WASTE WALK (EVEN WITHOUT A BADGE):
- Walk through any process you're involved in (at work, home, or volunteer)
- Identify waste: waiting, rework, unclear handoffs, unnecessary steps
- Ask: "If I could redesign this with no constraints, what would it look like?"

ACTION: Pick one process this month. Map it out. Eliminate one source of waste.

TOOL: Volunteer Leadership Blueprint
When people don't have to follow, you learn the essence of leadership.

- **Step 1:** Align Purpose—Remind people why the work matters

- **Step 2:** Share Ownership—Let volunteers design and lead pieces of the work
- **Step 3:** Recognize Contribution—Publicly highlight wins, big or small
- **Step 4:** Build Community—Create rituals of connection (check-ins, shout-outs, small celebrations)

APPLICATION: If you're in a volunteer or nonprofit role, commit to one recognition act per week.

CHAPTER 7

NAVIGATING NEW POWER STRUCTURES

Through my time with PMI, I got to interact with leaders from nearly every industry you could imagine. Technology, government, retail, healthcare—you name it, and project management had a footprint there. Because I served on the board in multiple roles, I wasn't just running events or sitting in meetings. I was sitting across the table from executives, senior managers, and community leaders who were shaping their organizations.

This is where I began to understand the art and science of networking—and more importantly, how to navigate power structures that had nothing to do with military rank.

NETWORKING AS ACTIVE LISTENING

For a long time, I thought networking was about showing up to an event, shaking hands, trading business cards, and hoping someone would remember you later. That's what most people think it is. But over the years, I discovered that real networking is more like active listening.

In active listening, you don't listen just to respond—you listen to understand. Networking, for me, became the same thing. When I met someone new, I wasn't focused on making an "ask" or pushing my agenda. Instead, I listened carefully, trying to understand their story, their needs, their frustrations. And then I asked myself: *Who do I know in my network who could help this person?*

It took years to build a network deep enough to work that way, but it changed everything. My style of networking wasn't transactional—it was relational. I wasn't keeping score or looking for immediate payback. I was building trust. And in the process, I found that opportunities had a way of finding me.

THE GOVERNMENT "HOLY GRAIL"

One of those opportunities came in the form of what most military retirees see as the ultimate prize: a government job. For many of us, that's the dream after leaving the service. The systems are familiar, the pace is comfortable, and the people around you often wore the same uniform not too long ago. It feels like a continuation of the community you just left.

So, like many of my peers, I stepped into a government role. On paper, it was perfect: stability, benefits, and a clear structure. But almost immediately, I felt the same frustration I had experienced in the Navy. Promotions were tied to time in grade, not performance. You could do great work, but unless the system decided you were "ready," you stayed put.

For someone who had spent ten years stuck at E5 in the Navy, I couldn't stomach the idea of going through that cycle again. The pace was too slow. The structure is too rigid. The advancement is too dependent on waiting instead of earning.

So I did the unthinkable: I left the security of a government job. I became a contractor.

TAKING THE RISK

In the hierarchy of government work, active-duty service members are at the top of the culture, GS employees are seen as the steady backbone, and contractors—well, contractors are often dismissed as "hired guns." People assume you're only in it for the paycheck. And yes, the pay is better—substantially better—but it comes with risk. Contracts expire. Budgets shift. Needs change. And when they do, you can be gone in an instant.

Security vs. opportunity. Stability vs. growth. For me, it wasn't a choice at all. I had already sacrificed too many years waiting on systems to validate me. This time, I wanted my performance—not my patience—to determine my future.

A JOB THROUGH A BEER AND AN EMAIL

The way I landed my first contract job says everything about the power of networking. While serving on the PMI board, we didn't have a formal job board at that time, so opportunities were shared by email. Someone would send out an opening, and board members would either apply to it themselves or pass it along to their networks.

One of those emails came through about a role in the

medical field. At first, I ignored it. The description didn't sound like a fit, and I moved on. A month later, the same email came back through. This time, the sender added a note: "My friend is still looking for someone to fill this role." Out of courtesy, I opened it again.

To my surprise, the job was pure project management—exactly the work I was doing already. I called the friend who had circulated the email, and by sheer coincidence, he was sitting in a bar with the hiring manager. He said, "Come down and meet him."

That was a Wednesday. We shook hands over a beer, talked about the contract, and by Sunday, the company had officially won the award. I applied Monday. By the following Wednesday, I had two interviews. By Thursday, I had a job offer.

All because of one email. All because of one connection. All because of networking.

FROM PROJECT TO PROGRAM

I started on the contract as a project manager, learning the ropes of the government contracting world. For two years, I focused on delivery—making sure projects were completed on time and within budget. But before long, I was promoted to program manager.

Now, instead of managing a single project, I was managing project managers. I was responsible for a portfolio worth $5.4 million. To some, that might not sound like much in the government contracting world, but to me, it was massive. Suddenly, I wasn't just leading teams—I was responsible for profit and loss, client satisfaction, hiring and firing decisions, and keeping the company's promises.

This was the commercial side of project management. It wasn't just about mission success—it was about financial performance, customer relationships, and reputation. It was high stakes, and for the first time since leaving the Navy, I felt the rush of real advancement.

The best part? Promotions came quickly, not because of a time-in-grade requirement, but because I delivered results. If I performed, I moved up. If I exceeded expectations, the rewards followed. It was merit-based, and after years of waiting for systems to notice me, that freedom was exhilarating.

LEARNING THE BUSINESS OF INFLUENCE

In the contracting world, influence operates differently. In the military, influence flowed through rank and command structure. In PMI, it flowed through service and relationships. In government contracting, it flowed through performance and value creation.

As a program manager, I had to navigate multiple stakeholders with competing priorities. The client wanted maximum capability for minimum cost. My company wanted maximum profit for minimum risk. My project managers wanted clear direction and adequate resources. My team wanted meaningful work and fair compensation.

Balancing these competing interests required a completely different kind of leadership. I couldn't order anyone to do anything. I had to negotiate, persuade, and align interests. I had to build coalitions of support for decisions. I had to manage up, across, and down simultaneously.

This taught me that modern leadership is less about having power and more about understanding how power works in different contexts. Every organization has formal authority structures and informal influence networks. The best leaders learn to navigate both.

THE ART OF CLIENT RELATIONSHIPS

Managing a $5.4 million portfolio also meant managing client relationships at a level I had never experienced. These weren't just customers—they were partners whose success determined my success. Their budgets determined my team's future. Their satisfaction determined my company's reputation.

I learned to think like a business owner, not just a project manager. Every decision had to consider not just immediate impact, but long-term relationships. Every challenge was an opportunity to demonstrate value and build trust. Every success was a chance to expand the partnership.

This perspective shift was crucial. Instead of seeing myself as someone who executed projects, I began seeing myself as someone who solved business problems through project execution. That reframing changed how I approached everything from resource allocation to team development to client communication.

POLITICAL NAVIGATION

The government contracting world also introduced me to organizational politics in ways the military never had. In the Navy, politics existed, but they were secondary to the mission and chain of command. In contracting, politics were part of the business model.

I had to learn to read rooms differently. Who were the real

decision-makers? What were the unspoken agendas? How did informal relationships affect formal processes? Where were the landmines, and how could I navigate around them while still achieving objectives?

This wasn't about manipulation or gamesmanship—it was about understanding systems and working within them effectively. I learned to build relationships before I needed them, to give credit generously, and to position wins in ways that made everyone look good.

One of my biggest breakthroughs came when I realized that successful leaders in complex organizations don't fight the system—they learn to work with it so effectively that they can shape it from within.

LONG-GAME LEADERSHIP

The contracting experience taught me about long-game leadership—the kind of influence that builds over time through consistent performance and relationship investment. Unlike military leadership, where authority was immediate and explicit, civilian influence had to be earned through demonstrated value.

I learned to think in cycles longer than individual projects. How could I position my team for future opportunities? What capabilities did we need to develop to stay competitive? How could we build such strong client relationships that we became indispensable partners rather than replaceable vendors?

This required patience and strategic thinking that the military's immediate-feedback culture hadn't demanded. In the Navy, you knew quickly whether you had succeeded or failed. In business, success often took months or years to materialize, and failure could be equally slow to reveal itself.

BUILDING SYSTEMS THAT SCALE

As my responsibilities grew, I had to transition from doing the work to building systems that enabled others to do the work. This meant developing processes, training programs, and quality standards that helped maintain excellence without my direct oversight.

I created project management frameworks that new hires could follow. I built client relationship protocols that ensured consistent service regardless of who was managing the account. I developed reporting systems that gave leadership visibility into performance without creating an administrative burden for project managers.

This systems thinking became one of my most valuable skills. Instead of being the person who could manage any project, I became the person who could build systems that enabled others to manage projects excellently. The shift from individual contributor to system builder was another form of leadership evolution.

CHAPTER 7 PLAYBOOK
STRATEGIC LEADERSHIP

NAVIGATING POWER STRUCTURES BEYOND DIRECT command requires mastering influence through value creation and relationship investment. Here's the framework that guided my transition from military authority to civilian influence:

THE THREE DIMENSIONS OF STRATEGIC INFLUENCE

1. Relational Networking

- Listen to understand, not to respond
- Connect others before connecting yourself
- Build trust through service, not self-promotion

Framework: The Network Value Audit

- **Monthly:** *Who did I help connect with someone else?*
- **Quarterly:** *What value did I create for others without expecting a return?*
- **Annually:** *How has my network grown in depth, not just breadth?*

Practical Tool: The 3-2-1 Networking Rule

- **3 Questions:** When you meet someone, ask three genuine questions about them
- **2 Connections:** Think of two people or resources you can connect them with
- **1 Follow-Up:** Within 24–48 hours, send one follow-up email or message

2. Performance-Based Credibility

- Deliver results consistently before seeking advancement
- Exceed expectations to build reputation capital
- Use success to create opportunities for others

Framework: The Credibility Cycle

- Promise conservatively and deliver generously
- Document and communicate successes appropriately
- Share credit widely, while taking responsibility personally

3. Political Intelligence

- Understand formal authority and informal influence networks
- Build relationships before you need them
- Navigate complexity without compromising integrity

Framework: The Power Map

- *Who are the real decision makers in this situation?*
- *What are the unspoken agendas and interests?*
- *How can I align my objectives with others' success?*

Quick Reference: Leading Through Influence

In complex organizations:

- Map both formal and informal power structures
- Build coalitions of support for important decisions
- Give others credit for shared successes
- Communicate value in terms others understand

When building credibility:

- Deliver on small commitments to earn larger opportunities
- Solve problems others can't or won't solve
- Make others successful, and they'll invest in your success
- Document impact in ways that matter to stakeholders

For long-term influence:

- Invest in relationships before you need them
- Build systems that create value beyond your direct involvement

- Develop others who will advocate for you when you're not present
- Think in cycles longer than immediate projects or assignments

Reflection Questions:

- How am I creating value for others without expecting immediate return?
- What systems can I build that will work without my direct oversight?
- Who are the informal influencers I need to understand and connect with?
- How can I position my work to support others' success?

THE STRATEGIC LEADERSHIP MINDSET

Leading without direct authority requires shifting from commanding compliance to creating conditions where others choose to support your objectives. This happens through consistent value creation, strategic relationship building, and having the wisdom to understand how influence works in different organizational contexts.

The goal isn't to accumulate power, but to generate results through others' willing cooperation. When people see you as someone who helps them succeed, they'll naturally want to help you succeed as well.

CHAPTER 8
THE PERFECT STORM

SOME SEASONS OF GROWTH DON'T ARRIVE WITH A whisper—they crash in like a wave, daring you to stay on your feet. For me, that season started in October. What followed was the most intense year of my professional life, where every title came with ten times the weight—and no instruction manual.

A TRIPLE THREAT

In October, I was promoted from Project Manager to Program Manager. Suddenly, I wasn't just accountable for my work—I was responsible for an entire $5.4 million federal contract; eight project managers now reported to me; and I was overseeing staffing, budgeting, compliance, delivery, and client relationships. The learning curve wasn't steep—it was vertical.

A month later, in November, my organization landed the largest transformation initiative in its history: an enterprise-wide project that would reshape everything from workflows to culture. And they picked me to lead it. Initially, this required 2-3 meetings a week lasting 4-5 hours each. Just to get all the stakeholders aligned with the new direction of the organization.

By January, I was elected President of the Hampton Roads Chapter of the Project Management Institute (PMI), overseeing 1,500 members and a volunteer board. Financials, governance, events, and community engagement—all of it now sat on my desk.

It felt like three full-time jobs, and I had one body to do them.

WHEN ACHIEVEMENT BECOMES SURVIVAL

People love titles. They celebrate the promotions, the LinkedIn updates, the applause. But they don't see the 4:30 a.m. emails, the dinner eaten out of a car, or the quiet breakdowns in parking lots between meetings.

This was more than the workload—it was identity pressure. I was supposed to be the guy who could handle it all. But some days, I was barely holding it together.

Leadership doesn't mean you don't struggle. It just means you can't struggle in silence.

Eventually, I stopped trying to outwork the chaos. Instead, I decided to **outstructure it**.

AT PMI: TAKING BACK TIME

Our board meetings ran over two hours—full of status updates and sidebar conversations. I introduced "reporting by exception:" if it's in the slide deck, we don't need to read it aloud. You only speak if:

- Something's off track
- You need a decision
- You need help from someone else

This one change gave everyone their time back—including me.

ON THE FEDERAL CONTRACT: LETTING GO OF THE HERO COMPLEX

At first, I wanted to touch every decision, every update. But that only slowed us down. I shifted from being the problem-solver to being the system-builder:

- I automated status updates
- I empowered PMs to own their decisions
- I required updates to come with proposed solutions

The result? More ownership, better execution, and fewer late-night fire drills.

ON THE ENTERPRISE TRANSFORMATION: BUILDING RHYTHM FROM CHAOS

This project couldn't be muscled through—it had to be managed with intention. I implemented:

- Weekly "drumbeat" meetings: same day, time, and format
- Standard dashboards for every workstream

- A clearly defined finish line, so we all knew what success looked like

When the system made sense, panic disappeared—and progress replaced it.

LESSONS FROM THE STORM

That year tested everything I thought I knew about leadership. But it also redefined it for me.

- **You don't rise to your goals—you fall to your systems.**
- **Delegation isn't giving up—it's giving others a chance to lead.**
- **People need direction, not control.**
- **Faith and structure can carry you when energy and clarity fade.**

That season didn't break me—it built me.

CHAPTER 8
PLAYBOOK THE PERFECT STORM

This chapter is about how to lead when your responsibilities multiply faster than your resources.

USE THESE TOOLS: When you're in over your head and need to create structure in the chaos.

1. PROTECT YOUR TIME

TOOL: Reporting by Exception

- Only bring up issues that require a decision, are off track, or need help.
- Skip redundant updates already documented in reports.

ACTION: Start your next meeting by asking: "Does anyone have exceptions to report?"

2. STOP BEING THE HERO

TOOL: Delegation Ladder

- Ask yourself: "Is this something only I can do?"
- If not, delegate—with clear expectations and trust.

ACTION: Identify one decision or task you're hoarding. Train someone else to own it.

3. CREATE RHYTHM IN CHAOS

TOOL: Drumbeat Meetings

- Same day, same time, same format each week.
- Structure: What happened last week? What's next? Where are the blocks?

ACTION: Set a recurring weekly meeting and enforce a standard structure.

4. MAKE SUCCESS VISIBLE

TOOL: Defined Finish Line

- Don't just say, "Complete the transformation."
- Define what "done" looks like, how it's measured, and by when.

ACTION: Write your project's finish line in one sentence. Share it weekly.

5. LEAD WITH HUMILITY AND FAITH

TOOL: Quiet Alignment

Morning mantra: "Give me strength for what's mine to carry, and wisdom for what's not."

ACTION: Start each day with a 60-second alignment—what do I need to carry, delegate, or let go?

KEY TAKEAWAYS

Being overwhelmed doesn't mean you're weak. It means you're human. The goal isn't to do more—it's to lead better. Build systems, trust your people, protect your energy, and remember: storms don't always sink the ship—sometimes they reveal who's ready to steer.

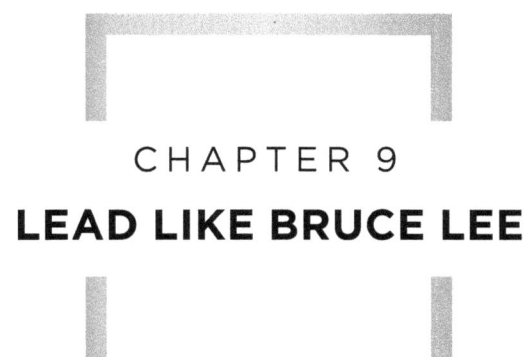

CHAPTER 9
LEAD LIKE BRUCE LEE

THE LEADERSHIP HACK NO ONE EXPECTS

When clients ask me for one leadership hack they can take back to the office and use right away, my answer usually surprises them. I tell them: Lead like Bruce Lee.

Now, before you HR types get nervous, let me explain. I'm not talking about karate chopping your teammates. I'm talking about Bruce Lee's philosophy of adaptability, resilience, and innovation—the very qualities leaders need today.

THE BRUCE LEE LESSON

Bruce Lee began his martial arts journey studying Wing Chun. He became highly skilled, but in a famous match against another Wing Chun expert, Bruce was frustrated. He won, but the fight took far too long. To Bruce, "winning slow" was almost as bad as losing.

So he did what all innovators do—he broke the mold.

Bruce went home, studied other forms of combat, and pulled the best from each discipline: boxing's footwork, fencing's timing, aikido's flow, judo's leverage. He combined them into a new style called Jeet Kune Do—the "Way of the Intercepting Fist."

It wasn't just a fighting system. It was a philosophy: Absorb what is useful. Discard what is not. Add what is uniquely your own.

This mindset allowed Bruce Lee to walk into any fight with options. He was no longer bound by tradition. He was free.

LEADERSHIP IN A MULTIGENERATIONAL WORLD

Now let's fast-forward from the ring to the workplace. Today's leaders face an equally complex environment. We're leading teams that are multigenerational—Baby Boomers, Gen X, Millennials, Gen Z—all working side by side, each with different values: stability versus flexibility, structure versus autonomy, loyalty versus purpose.

Add to that cultural diversity, remote work, and shifting technologies, and you've got the leadership equivalent of stepping into the ring with five different fighters at once.

The problem? Too many leaders are still trying to win every fight with one move. Command-and-control leaders only know how to push harder. Consensus leaders only know how to gather input. Servant leaders only know how to give. Coaching leaders only know how to ask.

But what happens when the situation calls for something different? Just like Bruce Lee discovered, sticking with one rigid style is a recipe for frustration.

YOUR LEADERSHIP: JEET KUNE DO

This is where the philosophy of Leading Like Bruce Lee comes in. Leadership, like combat, requires options. It requires adaptability. It requires the courage to step outside the boundaries of tradition, absorb what works, discard what doesn't, and add your own authenticity.

Think of leadership styles as tools in a bag:

- Visionary leadership sets the direction.
- Coaching leadership develops people.
- Servant leadership builds trust.
- Transformational leadership inspires change.
- Transactional leadership ensures accountability.

Each of these has value—but none of them, alone, is enough. Just like Bruce Lee blended martial arts into Jeet Kune Do, you must blend leadership approaches into your own style.

A NAVY EXAMPLE: WHEN "ONE MOVE" WOULDN'T WORK

I learned this lesson in the Navy. Early in my career, I thought being the toughest guy in the room would always win respect. It worked with some junior sailors who responded to discipline, but it backfired with others, who shut down or disengaged.

Later, when I led diverse teams, I realized the power of adapting my approach. With one sailor, I had to be a coach. With another, I had to be a mentor. With another, I had to be direct and firm. Same leader—different approach. That flexibility was the difference between compliance and commitment.

In leadership, as in combat, rigidity is weakness. Adaptability is strength.

THE OUTBOXED LEADER AS MARTIAL ARTIST

Throughout my journey—from the Navy to the warehouse, from PMI to contracting, from failure to reinvention—I've had to constantly adapt my leadership style. Each environment demanded different approaches, different tools, different ways of connecting with people.

In the military, structure and authority were the foundation. In the warehouse, I had to learn influence without rank. In PMI, I discovered the power of facilitation and service. In contracting, I mastered the art of stakeholder alignment and value creation.

Each experience added to my leadership toolkit. Like Bruce Lee combining martial arts disciplines, I combined leadership approaches from every environment I encountered. The result wasn't confusion—it was clarity. I became a leader who could adapt to any situation because I wasn't locked into any single style.

This is what it means to live Outboxed: refusing to be contained by traditional categories or conventional approaches. An Outboxed leader doesn't ask, "What's my leadership style?" They ask, "What does this situation require, and which tools do I need to use?"

THE FRAMEWORK: HOW TO LEAD LIKE BRUCE LEE

Here's how you build your own Leadership Jeet Kune Do:

1. Absorb What Is Useful

Study leadership frameworks. Read biographies. Watch leaders in action. Borrow practices that fit your context. For example, daily huddles in agile, one-on-ones from coaching, recognition practices from servant leadership. Think of yourself as a collector of techniques, not a disciple of just one.

2. Discard What Is Not Useful

Don't hold onto habits that slow you down. Eliminate outdated practices like annual-only feedback, rigid hierarchies, or "that's how we've always done it." Like Bruce Lee, be willing to challenge tradition—even if it makes others uncomfortable.

3. Add What Is Uniquely Your Own

Inject your personality, your values, and your story into your leadership. For me, my Navy background taught me the power of discipline and accountability. My corporate career taught me the value of collaboration and innovation. My faith taught me humility and purpose. Combined, they became my authentic style. Your unique blend is what makes you memorable and trustworthy as a leader.

THE EVOLUTION CONTINUES

What I've discovered over decades of leadership is that the best leaders never stop evolving. They're students for life, constantly learning new approaches, discarding what no longer serves them, and refining their authentic style.

This doesn't mean being inconsistent or unpredictable. It means being responsive. It means reading the room, understanding the people, and choosing the right tool for the right moment.

When I coach executives now, I don't teach them one leadership style. I help them build their own Leadership Jeet Kune Do. I help them identify their natural strengths, recognize their blind spots, and develop the flexibility to lead effectively in any situation.

Some days, you need to be the visionary casting a compelling future. Other days, you need to be the coach developing someone's potential. Sometimes, you need to be the servant leader building trust. Other times, you need to be the decisive executive making the tough call.

The key is knowing which approach the moment demands and having the skills to execute it authentically.

THE MULTIPLIER EFFECT

Here's what happens when you lead like Bruce Lee: you create other adaptive leaders. When your team sees you flexibly responding to different situations, they learn to do the same. When they see you absorbing new ideas, discarding what doesn't work, and adding your own innovations, they begin to develop their own leadership styles.

This is how you build organizations that can thrive in complexity and change. Not by creating followers who mimic your single style, but by developing leaders who can think, adapt, and innovate on their own.

Remember the principle from earlier in this book: the true sign of a leader isn't how many people they lead, but how many leaders they create. Leading like Bruce Lee accelerates this process because you're not just modeling one way to lead—you're modeling the mindset of continuous learning and adaptation that creates leaders.

This philosophy—this refusal to be contained by any single approach—is the essence of living Outboxed. It's the thread that runs through every chapter of this book, from the poverty of my childhood to the structure of the Navy, from the chaos of transition to the clarity of purpose I've found today.

Everything I've learned, every environment I've navigated, every failure I've endured, every success I've achieved—it all pointed to this truth: adaptability isn't just a leadership skill. It's the leadership skill that makes all others possible.

CHAPTER 9
PLAYBOOK LEAD LIKE BRUCE LEE

USE THIS AS A PRACTICAL EXERCISE TO BUILD YOUR own Leadership Jeet Kune Do:

STEP 1: AUDIT YOUR LEADERSHIP BAG

Write down the leadership styles you tend to use most (e.g., authoritative, coaching, servant, democratic, transformational). Circle the one you overuse. (That's your "Wing Chun.")

ACTION: Be honest about your default. If you always coach when you should decide, or always command when you should listen, you've found your starting point.

STEP 2: IDENTIFY GAPS

ASK: Where have I been stuck because my style didn't work? Which tools do I need to learn (e.g., more listening, more decisiveness, more vision)?

Reflection Questions:
- When did my default style fail me recently?
- What approach might have worked better?
- Which leadership "martial arts" am I missing from my toolkit?

STEP 3: BUILD YOUR JEET KUNE DO

Choose 1–2 new practices to try in the next 30 days.

EXAMPLES:
- If you're always directive, practice asking open-ended questions instead
- If you're always collaborative, practice making a quick decision solo
- If you avoid conflict, practice having one difficult conversation
- If you're always serious, practice injecting humor and connection

ACTION: Write down the specific practice and commit to trying it at least 5 times this month.

STEP 4: TEST AND ADAPT

Pay attention to outcomes. Did your new "move" create a better result? Keep what works, discard what doesn't; refine and repeat.

QUESTIONS TO ASK AFTER EACH ATTEMPT:
- How did the team respond?
- What felt authentic vs. forced?
- What would I adjust next time?
- Is this tool worth keeping in my bag?

STEP 5: PAY IT FORWARD

Share this philosophy with your team. Encourage them to experiment with their own leadership styles. Remember: leadership is not just about building followers—it's about creating more leaders.

ACTION: In your next team meeting, share the Bruce Lee philosophy and ask: "What leadership approaches could we borrow from other teams or industries?"

The Daily Practice

Morning Question: What does today's situation require, and which leadership tools do I need?

Before your first meeting or major task, pause and ask:

- What's the context? (Crisis, development, celebration, planning?)
- What do these people need from me right now?

- Which "martial art" should I use?

Evening Reflection: Where did I adapt effectively today, and where did I default to old patterns?
   Take 5 minutes before bed:

- Write down one moment you adapted well
- Write down one moment you fell into old habits
- What will you try differently tomorrow?

Weekly Review: What new leadership technique will I experiment with this week?
   Every Sunday or Monday:

- Review your notes from the week
- Identify one new tool to practice
- Share your experiment with someone who can give you feedback

Monthly Assessment: How has my leadership toolkit expanded, and what gaps still need attention?
   At month's end:

- List new practices you've adopted
- Identify persistent blind spots
- Celebrate growth while staying humble about the journey ahead

THE BRUCE LEE MINDSET: A SUMMARY

"Absorb what is useful, discard what is not, add what is uniquely your own."
   Applied to leadership:

ABSORB: Study everything. Read widely. Observe constantly. Borrow freely.

DISCARD: Let go of what doesn't serve. Challenge tradition. Kill sacred cows.

ADD: Inject your personality, values, and story. Be authentically you.

LEADERSHIP NUGGET

Leadership isn't about mastering one style. It's about mastering adaptability. The best leaders, like Bruce Lee, are students for life—always learning, always adjusting, always ready for the next fight.

FINAL REFLECTION

If there's one chapter in this book I want you to return to, it's this one. Because everything else—the frameworks, the tools, the stories—they all flow from this central truth: leadership that lasts is leadership that adapts.

You can't control what challenges come your way. You can't control what generation you're leading or what culture you're navigating. But you can control whether you show up with one rigid move or a full toolkit of options.

That's the freedom Bruce Lee discovered. That's the freedom I found after years of trying to fit into boxes that were never meant to contain me. And that's the freedom available to you.

Lead like Bruce Lee. Live Outboxed.

CHAPTER 10
THE BIRTH OF OUTBOXED

PLANTING THE SEED

Right before I became a contractor, while I was still a GS employee, I knew I wanted something different. I had always carried an entrepreneurial mindset—even if I didn't yet understand what that meant. I wanted something of my own, something that wasn't dictated by rank, quotas, or timelines.

So, without much of a plan, I filed the paperwork and created an LLC. That was the birth of Outboxed.

At the time, it was little more than a name, a set of bylaws, and an idea. I didn't know what direction it would take—I only knew that I wanted to own something beyond a government paycheck.

Looking back now, I can see that this was Bruce Lee's philosophy in action—even before I fully understood it. I was refusing to be contained by the traditional path: military service to government job to retirement. I was creating space for something new, even though I didn't yet know what would fill that space.

The name itself—Outboxed—was perfect. It captured everything I had been doing my entire life: refusing to fit into other people's categories, breaking out of systems that tried to contain me, and finding new ways to lead when the old ways didn't work.

LEARNING FROM CONTRACTING

When I left the GS world and moved into contracting, the picture started to sharpen. As a program manager, I got to see the inside of the government contracting machine: pricing structures, proposals, profit margins, performance measures. I wasn't leading the whole strategy, but I was in the room—watching how the experts built contracts, structured re-bids, and protected profitability.

Even as a cog in a much bigger wheel, I was getting an education. I didn't realize it at the time, but I was quietly building the foundation for running my own business one day.

This was absorbing what was useful—Bruce Lee's first principle. I was a student in someone else's classroom, taking notes on every lesson: how to price services, how to manage risk, how to build client relationships, how to structure proposals, how to protect margins while delivering value.

My employer was paying me to learn their business. And I was learning it all.

DISCOVERING THE STAGE

At the same time, my involvement with the Project Management Institute Hampton Roads Chapter (PMIHR) was pulling me in a new direction. We constantly brought in speakers to talk about leadership, strategy, and growth.

Watching them, I thought, *I can do that.*

I had always been a student of leadership. I had stories to tell, frameworks to share, and lessons that could help people. So, I leaned into the world of public speaking. I joined Next Level Speakers, a program created by Jeremy Anderson and Eric Thomas—two dynamic and highly sought-after speakers.

Through them, I learned that speaking was more than storytelling—it was a business. I built a website, developed a demo reel, started doing free talks, and slowly grew toward paid gigs. Just using my name, Martin White, I began to shape an identity as a speaker.

This was where things started to click. Public speaking wasn't just about sharing my story—it was about testing ideas, building credibility, and creating a pipeline for deeper work.

Every question someone asked after a speech was a potential service offering. Every "Can you help us with this?" was a doorway into consulting. Speaking became the front door to my business, and I learned to walk through it with confidence.

CONSULTING AND COACHING

The more I spoke, the more people approached me for help—not just with inspiration, but with practical leadership and team challenges. That opened the door to consulting. I now had a better vision of what Outboxed could become.

Soon after, I earned certification as an Organizational Development Coach. Now, Outboxed wasn't just an idea—it was becoming a coaching and consulting practice. By day, I was a contractor and program manager; by night and weekend, I was a speaker, consultant, and coach.

It was exhausting—but it was also exhilarating.

Consulting helped me sharpen my own leadership style, but more importantly, it forced me to create frameworks that could be replicated and scaled in any organization. I couldn't just tell people what worked for me—I had to codify principles that would work for anyone.

That's when I developed one of my earliest and most enduring models: TRUSTT.

THE TRUSTT FRAMEWORK: TURNING EXPERIENCE INTO INTELLECTUAL PROPERTY

Here's what I learned about building a business while holding down a full-time job: you need frameworks. You need systems. You need something you can teach, replicate, and scale.

TRUSTT became that for me. It was an acronym that captured the foundation of every healthy team I'd ever been part of—and diagnosed the dysfunction in every broken one:

T = TIME. Leaders must spend real, quality time with their people—not just during annual evaluations, but consistently, to understand who they are and what drives them.

R = RESPECT. Respect is shown in how you treat people and value their time. If a meeting only takes 15 minutes, don't schedule 30. Honor people with accuracy and efficiency.

U = UNDERSTANDING. Teams thrive when they understand the WHY. If the Why is strong enough, they can endure any How. Leaders must constantly connect people to the mission and purpose.

S = SAFE SPACE. A true team allows people to show up as their full selves. That means creating an environment where mistakes can be admitted early, ideas can be voiced freely, and bad news can be shared without fear.

T = TRUST (OR TRANSPARENCY). Leaders must trust their teams enough not to micromanage and be transparent enough to admit when they don't have the answer. Saying, "I don't know, but I'll find out" is not weakness—it's integrity.

T = TEAMWORK. The final multiplier. None of the above matter without a team-first mindset.

The TRUSTT framework became a mirror for organizations. Wherever trust was missing, dysfunction thrived. Wherever trust was strong, teams flourished.

More importantly, it became *sellable*. I could walk into a boardroom, present TRUSTT, and within an hour, executives would see exactly where their culture was breaking down. It wasn't vague leadership theory—it was a diagnostic tool they could use immediately.

That's when I understood: frameworks aren't just teaching

tools—they're intellectual property. They're products. And if you can codify what you know into a repeatable system, you can build a business.

THE OUTBOXED PHILOSOPHY TAKES SHAPE

By now, you can see the pattern. Just like Bruce Lee's philosophy Outboxed was built on adaptability:

Absorb what is useful:

- **From the Navy:** discipline, accountability, systems thinking
- **From contracting:** business acumen, client relationships, proposal strategy
- **From PMI:** facilitation, volunteer leadership, networking
- From speaking programs: how to build a personal brand, how to monetize a message
- From coaching certification: frameworks, one-on-one development skills

Discard what is not useful:

- The need for rank to lead
- The belief that stability is safer than growth
- The idea that entrepreneurship requires a perfect plan
- The assumption that you have to choose between a paycheck and a passion
- Traditional business hours and work-life "balance"

Add what is uniquely your own:

- My story: from poverty to Chief, transition to reinvention
- My faith: Philippians 4:13 as a life compass

- My frameworks: TRUSTT and others that came from my unique experiences
- My style: direct, authentic, no-nonsense leadership with heart
- My mission: creating leaders, not followers

Outboxed wasn't just a business—it was the embodiment of a philosophy. It was proof that you don't have to fit into someone else's box to succeed. You can create your own.

JUGGLING THREE LIVES

By this stage, I was living in three worlds simultaneously:

- Contractor and program manager over a $5.4M contract
- Founder of Outboxed, exploring speaking, consulting, and coaching
- Family man trying to balance it all

It was busy, messy, and imperfect. But it was also the beginning of something much bigger.

For the first time in my life, I wasn't just serving inside someone else's system. I was building my own. The reality is that most entrepreneurs start this way. You don't quit your job and leap into the void. You build while you work. You test ideas on nights and weekends. You use your day job as a training ground, your side hustle as a laboratory, and your family as your anchor.

It's not glamorous. It's exhausting. Some weeks, you wonder if it's worth it.

But then someone tells you that your framework changed their organization. Or a leader you coached gets promoted.

Or a speech you gave inspires someone to take the leap they'd been afraid to take.

And you remember why you started.

THE ENTREPRENEURIAL SHIFT: FROM EXECUTION TO OWNERSHIP

Building Outboxed required me to make fundamental shifts in how I thought about work, value, and success:

1. From "Doing" to "Designing"

Stop being only the executor; start shaping systems. As a contractor, my job was to deliver projects. As an entrepreneur, my job was to design systems that could deliver results without me.

2. From "Rank" to "Value"

In business, no one cares about your old title; they care about the value you create. My Navy rank didn't matter. My GS grade didn't matter. What mattered was whether I could solve problems people were willing to pay to solve.

3. From "Security" to "Risk & Reward"

Paychecks are replaced by possibility. The upside is yours—so is the risk. Every contract could be my last. Every speaking gig could be my first. But every success was mine to keep and build on.

4. From "Self" to "Scalability"

Build something that works beyond your effort alone. If Outboxed only worked when I was in the room, it wasn't a business—it was a job. Frameworks, systems, and training others became essential.

These shifts didn't happen overnight. They happened through hundreds of small decisions, failed experiments, and lessons learned the hard way.

But each shift moved me closer to something I had been chasing my entire life: the freedom to lead on my own terms.

KEY LESSONS FROM OUTBOXED'S BIRTH

Looking back at how Outboxed came to be, here's what I want you to take away:

Start before you're ready. Creating Outboxed before I had a plan gave me a container to grow into. Don't wait for clarity—create the structure first, then figure out what to put in it.

Every role is an education. Contracting taught me how business works—even when I was "just" a cog in the wheel. Use your current job as a classroom for your future business.

Speaking is more than a stage. It's a business, and it can open doors to coaching, consulting, and influence. If you can speak, you can build a pipeline to deeper work.

Frameworks multiply impact. TRUSTT wasn't just a tool for me—it became a way to replicate leadership lessons across organizations. Codify what you know. Turn experience into intellectual property.

Building your own system is messy—but worth it. Progress doesn't come from waiting for clarity. It comes from moving while you learn. Embrace the chaos. Test. Fail. Adjust. Keep going.

THE APPLICATION OF PHILOSOPHY

This chapter is the proof of concept for everything I wrote about in the previous chapter—it's a practical roadmap for building something from nothing.

I absorbed everything useful from every environment I'd been in. I discarded what didn't serve my mission. And I added what was uniquely mine—my story, my frameworks, my voice, my faith.

The result was Outboxed: a business, yes, but also a way of life. A brand built on the idea that you don't have to accept the boxes others put you in. You can create your own definition of success, your own path to impact, your own way of leading.

If you're reading this and you've been waiting for permission to start something, here it is: you don't need permission. You don't need a perfect plan. You don't need to have it all figured out.

You just need to file the paperwork, create the container, and start moving.

The rest will come.

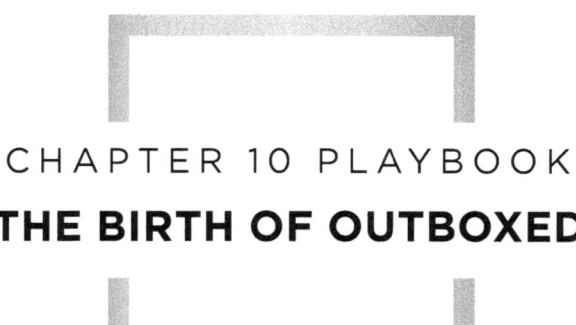

CHAPTER 10 PLAYBOOK
THE BIRTH OF OUTBOXED

This chapter captures the messy, exciting birth of Outboxed—juggling contracts, speaking, coaching, and family while laying the foundation of an enduring business. The playbook turns those lessons into tools you can use to build your own.

1. PLANTING THE SEED: FROM IDEA TO ENTITY

TOOL: The 3D Startup Checklist

- **Define:** Write one sentence about what problem you want to solve
- **Decide:** Choose a legal structure (LLC, S-Corp, Sole Proprietor) and file paperwork
- **Document:** Open a business bank account, get an EIN, and create a basic record-keeping system

ACTION: Even without clarity, create the container for your idea. Businesses grow into structure—they rarely start fully formed.

WHY THIS WORKS: Having a legal entity forces you to take your idea seriously. It creates psychological commitment and opens doors (like business banking and contracts) that aren't available to "hobbyists."

2. LEARNING WHILE YOU EARN

TOOL: The Shadow CEO Journal

During your day job, keep a notebook. Track:

- How leaders make decisions
- How budgets/contracts are structured
- Common mistakes and how they're fixed
- Processes that work well vs. those that waste time

At the end of each week, ask: *How would I do this if it were my business?*

ACTION: Use your employer as a classroom for entrepreneurship. Every meeting is a case study. Every project is a lesson in execution.

REAL TALK: Your employer is paying you to learn their business. Take notes. Ask questions. Watch everything. When you start your own business, you'll thank yourself for this education.

3. FINDING YOUR VOICE: FROM SPEAKING TO CONSULTING

TOOL: Speaker-to-Consultant Pipeline

- **Step 1:** Track every question people ask you after a speech (those are potential consulting services)
- **Step 2:** Turn the most common 2-3 questions into workshops or guides
- **Step 3:** Offer free sessions at first, then transition into fee-based services once you've proven results

ACTION: Speaking is marketing. Consulting is monetization. Link them.

THE MONEY MOVE: Don't just give speeches—give speeches that lead to paid work. End every talk with a clear next step for people who want to go deeper.

4. FRAMEWORK DEVELOPMENT

TOOL: The 5-Question Framework Builder

Ask yourself:

1. What recurring problem do I see in organizations?
2. What principle fixes it?
3. Can I explain it in 1-2 words?
4. Can I make it memorable with an acronym or metaphor?
5. Can I show results from applying it?

ACTION: Package your insights into repeatable frameworks. They build credibility and scale your message.

EXAMPLE: TRUSTT wasn't created in a vacuum—it came from years of seeing teams succeed or fail based on the same patterns. When I could name those patterns and give them structure, I had a product.

5. BALANCING MULTIPLE IDENTITIES

TOOL: The Triple Calendar Method
- Day Job Calendar: Blocks for contract/program work
- Business Calendar: Time carved out for speaking, consulting, coaching
- Family Calendar: Protected, non-negotiable blocks for family

Overlay them weekly to spot conflicts before they happen.

ACTION: Prevent burnout by planning across roles—not in isolation.

PRO TIP: Color-code your calendars. Red for day job, blue for business, green for family. When you see too much of one color, rebalance.

6. THE ENTREPRENEURIAL MINDSET AUDIT

TOOL: The Four Mindset Shifts Checklist
Where are you on each shift?

From → To | Where I Am Now (1-10)
1. From Doing to Designing ____
2. From Rank to Value ____

3. From Security to Risk & Reward ____
4. From Self to Scalability ____

ACTION: Be honest about where you are. You don't have to be at 10 on everything—but you do need to be moving in the right direction.

7. THE BRUCE LEE BUSINESS TEST

TOOL: Absorb, Discard, Add Assessment

What am I absorbing? (List 3-5 things you're learning from your current environment that will serve your future business)

What am I discarding? (List 3-5 beliefs, habits, or approaches that won't serve you as an entrepreneur)

What am I adding? (List 3-5 things that are uniquely yours—your story, values, style, frameworks)

ACTION: Review this monthly. Entrepreneurship is an ongoing practice of absorbing, discarding, and adding.

Quick Reference: The Outboxed Entrepreneur

When building a business while working full-time:

- File the paperwork first—clarity comes later
- Use your day job as entrepreneurship school
- Speaking opens doors to consulting and coaching
- Frameworks = intellectual property = sellable products
- Keep an updated and balanced calendar; prioritize your family

When developing your unique offering:

- Absorb best practices from every environment
- Discard what doesn't fit your mission or values
- Add your authentic story, style, and frameworks
- Make it memorable (acronyms, metaphors, visuals)
- Show results, not just theory

When balancing multiple identities:

- Color-code your calendars
- Protect family time
- Say No to some "good" opportunities to save space for great ones
- Accept that some seasons will be imbalanced—name them and set end dates

Key Takeaways

- Don't wait for the perfect plan—file the paperwork and create the container
- Use your day job as a training ground for entrepreneurship
- Public speaking isn't just storytelling—it's a business pipeline
- Frameworks like TRUSTT turn experience into intellectual property
- Balance requires intentional systems, not wishful thinking

CLOSING THOUGHT

The birth of Outboxed wasn't a single moment—it was a series of decisions to create space for something new, to learn from every environment, and to build while I earned.

It wasn't clean. It wasn't comfortable. But it was mine.

And that made all the difference.

If you're in that messy middle right now—working full-time while building something on the side—know this: you're not behind. You're exactly where you need to be. The work you're doing in the margins will become the foundation of everything you build.

Keep filing paperwork. Keep learning. Keep building frameworks. Keep speaking. Keep testing.

The container you're creating today will hold more than you can imagine tomorrow.

CHAPTER 11
THE LEADERSHIP LAB

I'VE WORKED IN MANY INDUSTRIES SINCE LEAVING THE Navy—from warehouse supervisor to instructor for the military, to government employee, to contracted project manager, to program manager leading a nonprofit organization. Looking back, I realize I've run the full gamut of industries and leadership levels.

At first, I thought I was simply chasing opportunity, or trying to find the right fit. But over time, I came to see that what I was really doing was building my own leadership laboratory. Each environment became an experiment—a place to test, observe, and refine what leadership looks like when the rules change.

Because, the truth is, leadership doesn't look the same everywhere.

Every job, every industry, every team is a new test case. And if you pay attention—if you treat each environment like a lab instead of just a paycheck—you learn things no classroom or textbook could ever teach you.

EXPERIMENT #1: THE WAREHOUSE FLOOR

The Philadelphia distribution center was my first real experiment in civilian leadership, and it was brutal. I had just retired from the Navy as a Senior Chief. For 26 years, I had led teams with the weight of rank behind me. People listened because they had to. Orders were orders. The chain of command was clear. But at that warehouse, six hours from my home in Virginia, none of that mattered.

I worked twelve-hour shifts on Friday, Saturday, and Sunday, then drove six hours each way to get back and forth. My weeks became a blur of highway asphalt, warehouse floors, and exhaustion. I missed family dinners, kids' activities, and simple time at home.

The Challenge: Leading Without Rank

At the distribution center, I faced an entirely new kind of challenge. These weren't sailors motivated by duty, country, or rank. These were men and women working for a paycheck, trying to get through their shifts and make ends meet. The "Because I said so" approach, which sometimes works in the military, fell flat here. Immediately.

I remember the first time I tried to pull rank on someone. I was managing a team unloading containers, and one worker was moving slower than I thought necessary. In the Navy, I would've said, "Pick up the pace, sailor," and that would've been the end of it.

Here? The guy looked at me and said, "If you don't like the way I work, there's three other warehouses within five miles. I can be working somewhere else by Monday."

That stopped me cold.

If they didn't like the job, they could quit and find another warehouse by the end of the week. I had no leverage. No rank. No authority they were obligated to respect.

I had to discover quickly: if you want people to follow, you have to inspire them—not order them.

The Work: Profiling and Process

I was hired as a "high potential" candidate with the idea that I would rotate through different parts of the distribution center and eventually move into management. And, to their credit, they kept their promise. I worked in receiving, processing, and shipping. I oversaw teams of thirty, balancing production quotas with the reality of people's energy and motivation.

One of the most eye-opening discoveries was learning how to "profile" the work: understanding what products were in the pipeline, how much could realistically be processed, and which team members had the right skills for the right tasks.

Moving 15,000 winter coats in the middle of June required a different rhythm than unloading containers of luggage or jewelry. It was part science, part art, and part negotiation.

I learned to read the flow. Some workers were better at heavy lifting. Others excelled at precision tasks. Some thrived with autonomy. Others needed more structure. My job wasn't to make everyone the same—it was to match the right person to the right work at the right time.

This was also where I was first introduced to Lean and Six

Sigma principles—concepts that would later become part of my professional DNA. Process improvement. Eliminating waste. Finding efficiency.

The Navy had given me discipline and mission focus, but this job taught me to see leadership through the lens of systems and processes. It wasn't enough to push harder—you had to design smarter.

The Leadership Lessons

The real challenge was leading people who didn't have to listen to me. And that forced me to develop three core skills:

Respect as Currency: I learned that respect in civilian work isn't automatic—it's earned. And the fastest way to earn it was to get on the floor and work beside them. When people saw me sweating next to them, moving boxes, and willing to do the hard stuff, they started listening.

Consistency Over Commands: Without the threat of rank-based punishment, the only thing that held teams together was consistency. If I said I'd do something, I did it. If I promised to fight for better conditions or fair treatment, I followed through. Trust built slowly, one kept promise at a time.

Motivation Through Meaning: I couldn't order compliance, so I had to help people see why the work mattered. Sometimes that was as simple as, "If we finish this shipment early, you get to go home." Other times, it was connecting the dots: "This coat you're processing? Someone's buying it for their kid this winter. We're not just moving boxes—we're making sure people get what they need."

The Cost

Still, the cost was high. My wife didn't want to move to Philadelphia. My kids needed me home. And the six-hour drives were draining my soul.

After two years, she gave me that ultimatum.

I chose my family.

Looking back, that warehouse was my crash course in humility. I had been a Senior Chief, commanding specialized teams in some of the Navy's most demanding environments, then suddenly, I was just another guy in steel-toed boots trying to move boxes and make a quota.

But it was also where I learned one of the most important leadership lessons of my life: influence without authority is the purest test of leadership.

When people don't have to follow you, when they can walk away at any moment, the only thing that keeps them there is your ability to inspire, serve, and show up with integrity.

EXPERIMENT #2: GOVERNMENT EMPLOYEE

After returning to Virginia and finishing my business degree, I landed a government job as a GS employee. On paper, it looked perfect—stability, benefits, clear structure, and familiar systems that mirrored the military.

The Challenge: Hierarchy and Patience

As a government employee—a GS—you learn quickly that the leadership style there mirrors the military in many ways.

The structure is hierarchical. Authority flows downward. Respect is demanded by rank as much as by ability. To get things done, you often rely on formal processes and chain of command. It's directive, orderly, and sometimes rigid.

For someone coming from the Navy, this felt comfortable. I understood hierarchy. I knew how to navigate bureaucracy. The language, the systems, the culture—it all made sense.

But here's what I quickly discovered: just like in the Navy, advancement wasn't based on performance alone. It was based on time in grade.

You could do exceptional work, deliver results ahead of schedule, and save your department money—but unless the system decided you were "ready" based on time served, you stayed put.

For someone who had spent ten years stuck at E5 in the Navy, this felt suffocating. I had left the military partially because I was tired of waiting for systems to notice me. Now here I was, in the same cycle.

The Leadership Lessons

Government work taught me important lessons, even in its rigidity:

Structure Creates Accountability: The systems were slow, but they were also fair in their own way. Everyone knew the rules. Everyone followed the same process. There was transparency in how things worked, even if that transparency sometimes revealed inefficiency.

Documentation Matters: In government work, if it's not documented, it didn't happen. I learned to track everything, create paper trails, and build cases with evidence.

This discipline would serve me well later in contracting and consulting.

Patience as Strategy: Sometimes, the best leadership move is waiting. Not because you're passive, but because you're strategic. I learned to plant seeds, build relationships, and position ideas months before they needed to be approved.

But I also learned this: some environments will never reward merit over tenure. And when you realize that, you have two choices—accept it or move on.

I moved on.

EXPERIMENT #3: NONPROFIT LEADERSHIP (PMI)

While working as a government employee and later as a contractor, I threw myself into volunteer leadership with the Project Management Institute (PMI) Hampton Roads Chapter. Over seven years, I served in multiple roles: Military Liaison Director, VP of Membership, VP of Operations, and eventually President of a 1,500-member chapter.

The Challenge: Leading Without Leverage

In a nonprofit, leadership has to be adaptive, relationship-driven, and deeply tied to the mission. You aren't ordering people to perform; you're inspiring them to volunteer. You aren't leveraging paychecks; you're appealing to passion. Success depends on whether you can ignite people's intrinsic motivation and rally them around a shared cause.

This was a completely different challenge than anything I'd faced before.

These were volunteers. They didn't have to show up. They didn't have to stay. If they felt unappreciated, underutilized, or uninspired, they could simply walk away—and there was nothing I could do about it.

I remember one board meeting where a key volunteer threatened to quit because he felt his contributions weren't being recognized. In the military, I would've reminded him of his commitment. In the corporate world, I might've referenced his contract or job description.

Here? I had nothing. No leverage. No power.

All I could do was listen, validate, and remind him why the work mattered. I had to make him feel seen, valued, and essential. And it worked—but only because the relationship was real, not transactional.

The Leadership Lessons

Align with Purpose, Not Paychecks: People volunteer because they believe in something. My job as a leader wasn't to manage tasks—it was to constantly reconnect people to the mission. "Why are we here? What difference are we making? How does your role matter?"

Recognition is Oxygen: In volunteer organizations, recognition isn't a nice-to-have—it's essential. People need to know their work matters. I learned to celebrate wins publicly, thank people often, and make sure no contribution went unnoticed.

Ownership Creates Commitment: The more I let volunteers lead their own initiatives, the more invested they became. Instead of assigning tasks, I invited people to design solutions. Instead of micromanaging, I trusted them to own outcomes.

Lead Through Questions: I discovered that asking the right questions was more powerful than giving the right answers. "What do you think we should do?" "How would you approach this?" "What would success look like?" These questions invited collaboration and creativity.

PMI taught me that leadership without authority is actually more powerful than authority without influence. When you can't rely on rank, title, or paycheck, you're forced to become the kind of leader people CHOOSE to follow.

EXPERIMENT #4: CONTRACTING WORLD

When I transitioned from government work to contracting, I entered yet another arena with its own unique dynamics.

The Challenge: Expert Autonomy

When I managed that $5.4 million contract, there were seven project managers reporting directly to me. These weren't junior employees who needed hand-holding; they were experts—many with decades of experience, advanced degrees, and specialized skills.

Contractors are, in many ways, hired guns. They're paid for expertise, but they live with constant uncertainty—the contract might not be renewed tomorrow. That uncertainty makes them both highly driven and highly cautious.

Leading in that space requires a delicate balance: don't micromanage experts, don't waste their time, but also make sure the quality of their work speaks for itself. The best approach I found was simple: let the experts be the experts.

Remove obstacles, provide direction when needed, but get out of their way.

I remember one contractor saying to me, "Just tell me what you want and leave me alone. I know how to do it right."

That stuck with me.

The Leadership Lessons

Trust Unlocks Performance: When I trusted my project managers to own their work, they delivered better results than if I had tried to control every detail. My job wasn't to tell them HOW—it was to clarify the WHAT and WHY, then let them work.

Clear Outcomes, Flexible Methods: I learned to define success clearly (deliverables, deadlines, quality standards), but leave the methods open. Different experts had different approaches, and that diversity strengthened our results.

Advocate, Don't Dictate: My role shifted from commander to advocate. I fought for resources, removed bureaucratic obstacles, and represented my team's interests to leadership. This built loyalty faster than any directive ever could.

Performance Speaks Louder Than Presence: In contracting, results matter more than face time. I stopped measuring productivity by hours worked and started measuring by outcomes delivered. This created a culture of ownership and accountability.

Contracting taught me that modern leadership is less about having power and more about understanding how power works in different contexts.

THE FLEXIBLE LEADER

These shifts taught me that leadership is not a fixed posture. It's a position you adjust depending on the environment and the people you serve.

- Sometimes, you lead from the front, setting the pace and showing others what "right" looks like.
- Sometimes, you lead from alongside, shoulder-to-shoulder, sharing the load and demonstrating solidarity.
- Sometimes, you lead from behind, giving others the spotlight, pushing them to grow, and quietly ensuring no one falls behind.

The trick is knowing what position to play at what time—and being comfortable in each position.

Too many leaders insist on being out front all the time. Others hide in the back and call it humility. True leadership is fluid. You can be in charge and still get your hands dirty. You can hold authority and still empower others.

It doesn't diminish your role. In fact, it proves you care.

LESSONS FROM THE LAB

Each role, each industry, each "experiment" in my leadership lab, gave me new insights:

Hierarchy teaches discipline. The military and government sharpened my respect for structure, accountability, and clear expectations. Although most companies have an organizational chart and they look like they have a hierarchy like the military and the government, I have found that most of them are not strict, or the culture is not one of simply following the orders of the person above you in the org chart. That's probably for the best, because most people don't function well in a highly-structured environment. So trying to impose a military-style structure in a commercial corporation would lead to seriously disgruntled workers and stifle the creativity of the team.

Nonprofits teach influence. You learn how to inspire rather than order, how to lead without paychecks as leverage. My favorite people to work with are the ones doing what they are passionate about. This is the purest form of leadership. People will either follow you or they won't—and the consequences of the second are usually minimal, so your abilities as a leader and your ability to inspire others are really tested.

Contract work teaches trust. You discover the power of letting experts do their jobs without suffocating oversight.

Warehouses teach humility. You learn that leadership isn't about titles or credentials—it's about showing up, working beside people, and earning respect through consistency and integrity.

And together, they all taught me that leadership isn't one-size-fits-all. It's a craft. A discipline. A laboratory where every failure, every success, every environment adds another layer of understanding.

THE LEADERSHIP LAB MINDSET

What I've come to realize is this: every job is a classroom if you're paying attention.

Most people go to work, do their job, and go home. They see their role as transactional—time for money, effort for paycheck.

But leaders see every environment as a laboratory. They ask:

- What's working here that I can replicate elsewhere?
- What's broken that I can learn to fix?
- How do people respond to different approaches?
- What would I do differently if this were my organization?

This mindset transforms every experience—even the frustrating ones—into data. And over time, that data becomes wisdom.

The warehouse taught me influence without authority. Government work taught me patience and documentation. Nonprofits taught me inspiration and recognition. Contracting taught me trust and autonomy.

None of these lessons came from books. They came from experiments. From trying things, failing, adjusting, and trying again.

That's what a leadership lab is: a willingness to treat every environment as a test case for growth.

CHAPTER 11 PLAYBOOK

THE LEADERSHIP LAB

The following tools and exercises help you test and refine your own leadership "lab results" in different contexts:

1. THE LAB NOTEBOOK

TOOL: Keep a running record of leadership experiments. Write down what you tried, what environment you were in, how people responded, and what you'd do differently. Over time, this builds your personalized "leadership lab manual."

I have a ton of notebooks from past projects and just day-to-day life on the job. Now I use them as my own personal manual.

ACTION STEP: Start with your current role. What's one leadership experiment you're running this week? Capture it in writing.

Example Format:

- Date & Context:
- What I Tried:
- How People Responded:
- What Worked:
- What Didn't:
- What I'll Try Next:

2. THE FRONT-SIDE-BACK DRILL

TOOL: Practice shifting positions. For one week, intentionally rotate how you lead your team. Spend one day leading from the front (visible direction), one day from the side (collaboration), one day from the back (delegation and support).

ACTION STEP: At the end of each day, journal how the team responded. Which posture unlocked the most productivity or morale?

Reflection Questions:

- When does my team need me to lead from the front?
- When do they need me shoulder-to-shoulder?
- When do they need me to step back?

3. INFLUENCE WITHOUT AUTHORITY

TOOL: In environments where you can't "order" results (nonprofits, cross-functional teams), practice persuasion through values. Build buy-ins by linking tasks to the mission.

ACTION STEP: Next time you need someone's effort without leverage, start your ask with, "This connects to our bigger purpose because..."

The Formula:
- ◆ **Context:** Acknowledge their reality
- ◆ **Connection:** Link to shared mission/values
- ◆ **Contribution:** Show how their work matters
- ◆ **Choice:** Respect their autonomy

4. THE EXPERT AUTONOMY CHECKLIST

TOOL: Before stepping into an expert's lane, ask three questions:

1. Do I understand this task better than they do?
2. Is my input removing a roadblock, or just adding noise?
3. Am I trying to control, or am I trying to support?

ACTION STEP: For one week, apply this checklist before giving direction to a highly skilled team member.

If your answer to #1 is No and #3 is "control"–step back. Your job is to clarify outcomes, not dictate methods.

5. MISSION VS. MECHANICS EXERCISE

TOOL: Separate what needs to be done (mission) from how it gets done (mechanics). Strong leaders define the "what" and let teams drive the "how."

ACTION STEP: Take your next project and write the mission on one page. On another page, let the team design the mechanics. Compare results—you'll likely see creativity you wouldn't have imagined.

Mission Statement Template:
- **Purpose:** Why this matters
- **Outcome:** What success looks like
- **Constraints:** Non-negotiables (budget, timeline, quality standards)
- **Freedom:** What the team can decide

6. THE WAREHOUSE TEST: LEADING WITHOUT LEVERAGE

TOOL: Remove all your usual sources of authority and ask: Would people still follow me?

Reflection Questions:
- If I had no title, would people listen to me?
- If I couldn't fire or promote anyone, could I still motivate them?
- If people could walk away at any time, would they choose to stay?

ACTION: Identify one area where you're relying too heavily on position power. Practice influence-based leadership there for 30 days.

7. CROSS-TRAINING LEADERSHIP STYLES

TOOL: Just like cross-training in fitness, practice leadership styles that don't come naturally to you.

- **If you're naturally directive:** Spend a week asking questions instead of giving answers
- **If you're naturally collaborative:** Practice making solo decisions quickly
- **If you're naturally hands-off:** Get in the details for one project
- **If you're naturally detail-oriented:** Delegate fully and trust the process

ACTION: Pick your opposite style. Practice it for two weeks. Journal what you learn.

Quick Reference: The Leadership Lab Mindset

When entering a new environment:

- Observe before acting
- Ask questions before making changes
- Identify informal power structures
- Learn the language and culture first

When leading without authority:

- Connect to the mission and purpose
- Build relationships before you need them
- Recognize contributions publicly and often
- Let people own their work

When leading experts:

- Clarify outcomes, not methods
- Remove obstacles, don't create them
- Trust first, verify results later
- Advocate for resources and support

When leading in hierarchy:

- Document everything
- Build cases with evidence
- Plant seeds months in advance
- Work the formal and informal systems

When testing a new approach:

- State your experiment clearly
- Give it a fair trial (at least 2–4 weeks)
- Collect feedback systematically
- Adjust based on results, not ego

KEY TAKEAWAYS

Leadership isn't static. It isn't about one style or one method that works everywhere. It's a lab—a constant experiment. The best leaders aren't rigid; they're adaptable, humble enough to learn, and bold enough to adjust.

Every environment you enter is an opportunity to test, observe, and refine what works. Some experiments will fail. That's expected. But if you're documenting the lessons, you're building a leadership manual that's uniquely yours—tested in real conditions, with real people.

The warehouse taught me humility and influence without authority. Government work taught me patience and systems thinking. Nonprofits taught me inspiration and purpose-driven leadership. Contracting taught me trust and expert autonomy.

None of these lessons came from theory. They came from doing the work, paying attention, and treating every environment like a laboratory.

That's the leadership lab Mindset: every job is a classroom, every challenge is an experiment, and every failure is data.

The question isn't whether you'll face different environments—you will. The question is whether you'll treat them as obstacles to endure or opportunities to learn.

Choose the lab. Choose growth. Choose adaptability.

That's how you become the kind of leader who can thrive anywhere.

CHAPTER 12
LEGACY—A LIFE UNCONTAINED

If you ever have to walk into a room, a meeting, or any space and ask, "Do you know who's in charge here?"—then it's probably not you. Real leadership doesn't have to announce itself. You can feel it when it's present.

I learned that lesson, not in a boardroom or on a ship, but in the small moments—watching my mother open her home to strangers, seeing Chief Bush invest in a sailor who didn't deserve it, and eventually, standing in front of teams who chose to follow me not because they had to, but because they wanted to.

Leadership isn't about volume or titles. It's about how people carry themselves after you leave. It's about what remains when your name isn't in the room anymore. That's legacy—not the kind carved in stone, but the kind etched quietly into people.

WHAT LEGACY REALLY MEANS

For most of my life, I thought legacy was what you built. A job title. A record of accomplishments. A résumé that made people nod their heads. But the older I get, the more I realize those things fade. Buildings collapse. Jobs are forgotten. Awards collect dust.

But people? People remember who you helped them become.

When I think about what I want to leave behind as a legacy, I don't think about titles, awards, or positions. I think about people. I want to leave behind a generation of leaders—not replicas of me, not people who lead exactly the same way I did—but individuals who can think critically, who show compassion, and who have enough emotional intelligence to understand what makes their teams thrive.

Leaders who know when to take charge, and, just as importantly, when to step aside and let others lead.

When I leave this earth—and I know one day I will—I don't want people to remember me as the guy who survived poverty, or sailed the world with the Navy, or ran a nonprofit, or started a company called Outboxed.

I want them to say something much simpler: "He helped me lead. He helped me believe I could."

Not lead like me. Not talk like me. Not copy my style. But think—truly think. Show compassion. Have the emotional intelligence to understand their people. And when the time comes, to step aside so someone else can rise higher.

THE MIRROR, NOT THE SPOTLIGHT

Some people think leadership is a spotlight. I believe real leadership is a mirror.

When others stand in front of you, do they see your greatness—or their own potential? I learned this from watching the leaders who shaped me. Chief Bush didn't parade his accomplishments—he invested time in me when I was stuck at E5, angry and directionless. Senior Chief Zicafoose didn't need to tell me she was a great leader—I felt it in how she created space for others to grow.

The best leaders I've known weren't the loudest voices in the room. They were the ones who made everyone else feel like they had a voice worth hearing.

MEASURING LEADERSHIP DIFFERENTLY

A lot of people see great leaders as the sum of their personal accomplishments. They look at what someone built, what they achieved, or how high they climbed. And yes, good leaders get things done. But I measure leadership differently.

I measure leadership by how many other leaders you've raised—how many people you've helped reach or even surpass your level.

I once read that if leadership were a scale of one to ten, and you were a five, you could never develop anyone beyond a five. I don't believe that. I believe a leader—even a "five"—can produce sixes, sevens, and tens if they care enough to nurture people early in their journey.

By understanding what motivates them. By helping them identify both their strengths and their weaknesses. By giving them the tools to grow—and then getting out of their way.

LETTING PEOPLE GO

You can't let your pride or your ego get in the way of someone else's growth. If another mentor, another environment, or another opportunity can help them grow faster or further—release them. That's not failure. That's love. That's leadership.

Too often, we hold on to people because we don't want to lose them. We convince ourselves it's about loyalty, but really it's about fear—the fear that we won't be as effective without them, that we'll lose our edge or our comfort.

But holding people back so you can keep them close is one of the most harmful things a leader can do. When you care about people, you want them to outgrow you. You want them to expand beyond what you could offer.

I saw this principle at work in my own career. When it was time for me to leave the Navy, some people questioned whether I would make it. But the leaders who truly cared about me said, "Go. There's more for you out there."

Years later, when talented people on my teams got offers to move to bigger opportunities, I did the same. I celebrated their growth, even when it meant my team would be weaker in the short term. Because that's what legacy looks like—helping people fly, not clipping their wings.

WHEN A LEADER'S WORK IS DONE

There's a quote I'm paraphrasing, but it stuck with me: "When a great leader's work is done, the people say, 'We did it ourselves.'"

That line always hits me. Because that's what great leadership looks like—it doesn't feel forced. It doesn't feel staged. When it's done right, it feels natural.

The team grows. The mission moves forward. The organization evolves. And nobody feels like they were pushed or tricked or micromanaged. Instead, they feel like they did it because they wanted to—because it mattered to them.

That's what I want to build. Environments where things happen naturally because people are engaged, empowered, and invested. When that happens, the culture sustains itself. It outlives any single person.

A CULTURE OF EXCELLENCE, NOT JUST AN EXCELLENT CULTURE

My father's death taught me something I didn't understand until decades later: the difference between an excellent culture and a culture of excellence. This is not just word play.

An excellent culture depends on certain people being in the room. A culture of excellence remains—even when they leave.

When my father died, our family's stability died with him. But my parents had also built something that did survive: values. Education wasn't encouraged—it was expected. Service wasn't admirable—it was normal. Faith wasn't forced—but it was the foundation. Those principles outlasted my father's death and shaped every one of his nine children. My parents had created a culture of excellence!

That's the culture I want to leave behind. Not my personality. Not my specific methods. But a philosophy that outlasts me:

- ◆ Do hard things.
- ◆ Leave people better than you found them.
- ◆ Let faith power your effort, not replace it.
- ◆ Prepare people to lead without you.

THE FAITH THAT GROUNDS ME

I don't push religion on anyone. But I also won't deny what's true for me: my strength, my patience, my ability to endure—all of it comes from God.

There's a scripture I've carried for years: "I can do all things through Christ who strengthens me." Not because I'm strong, but because I know what it feels like to be weak and still keep going.

Faith, to me, isn't about rules—it's about responsibility. If God trusted me with the experiences I've had—poverty, war, leadership, failure, restoration—then I don't get to keep that wisdom to myself. That's not faith. That's selfishness.

If I've been blessed with lessons, then I'm supposed to pass them on. Multiply them. Leadership is stewardship.

This book exists because I believe that. Every framework I've shared, every story I've told, every tool I've developed—they're not mine to hoard. They're meant to be given away, used, adapted, and passed on to the next generation of leaders.

RAISING LEADERS WHO RAISE LEADERS

I've seen too many leaders try to build empires so people remember their name. But empires fall. Egos crumble. The real test of leadership is this:

Do the people you led now lead others? And do those leaders teach someone else to lead after them?

If your influence dies with you, then it was popularity, not leadership.

I don't want clones of me. I want leaders who are smarter, wiser, and more compassionate than I ever was. And I want them to raise leaders even greater than themselves.

> **That's how legacy works. Not addition—multiplication.**

Five, ten, twenty years from now, I want the people I've led or mentored to be out there doing great things. I want them to occasionally look back and think about a conversation we had, a piece of advice I gave, or maybe just how I treated them—and see that as a small spark that helped them move forward.

That's the kind of legacy I care about. Not recognition. Not credit. Just impact.

GROWTH BY PROXIMITY

As leaders, parents, friends, and human beings, that's really what it's about:

- As a parent, you want to raise better humans than you were.
- As a business owner, you want to leave your company in a stronger position than when you found it.
- As a friend, you want people to grow just by being around you.

Growth by proximity—that's the test of real influence.

THREE QUESTIONS I ASK MYSELF NOW

As I step into this phase of life—father, husband, veteran, coach, student of leadership—these are the questions I return to:

1. If I walked away today, what would keep going?

Not the projects, but the principles.

2. Who have I coached that didn't just become a version of me, but became better?

Leadership is not replication—it's elevation.

3. What am I holding on to that I should be passing on?

Wisdom doesn't grow when you guard it. It multiplies when you give it away.

THE STUDENT, NOT THE MASTER

Like I said in the beginning of this book, I'm a student of leadership. It's a journey with no finish line. I'll always feel like there's more I could have done, something I could have said differently, a lesson I could have learned sooner.

I overanalyze. I revisit old situations and ask myself what I did right, what I did wrong, and how I can do better next time. That's not humility—that's reality. Leadership is too complex, people are too diverse, and circumstances change too rapidly for anyone to claim mastery.

If you ever start to believe you've reached the pinnacle of your leadership ability—or that you've mentored all the people you can—check your ego.

> **Leadership is not about mastery. It's about movement. It's about curiosity. It's about staying open enough to grow and humble enough to keep giving.**

Because the moment you stop learning, you stop leading.

A VISION THAT TRANSCENDS GENERATIONS

In the end, I want my leadership to transcend generations. I want the lessons, conversations, and examples I've shared to still mean something years from now. To still work. To still apply.

Because people, at their core, don't change that much. We all want to belong to something meaningful. We all want to contribute. We all want to win together.

That's what leadership is supposed to create—a space where those things happen naturally. That's the kind of legacy I want to leave behind: not a contained version of success, but an uncontained life vision. One that keeps expanding, growing, and evolving through the people I've had the privilege to lead.

And if I've done it right, those future leaders—the ones I helped guide, coach, or inspire—will keep my legacy alive by creating even better leaders than themselves.

That's how leadership lives on. Not through monuments or memories, but through motion. Through people. Through purpose that refuses to stop at one generation.

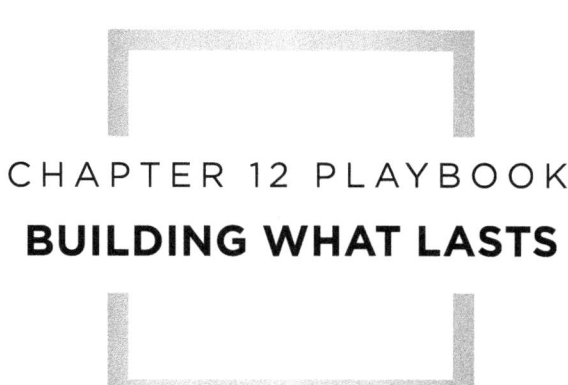

CHAPTER 12 PLAYBOOK
BUILDING WHAT LASTS

Legacy isn't built in a moment—it's built in a thousand small choices to invest in others. Here are the tools that will help you build leadership that outlasts you.

1. THE 5–10 PARADOX

TOOL: Assess your "leadership scale." Are you a 5 who's helping others reach 6, 7, or 10? The goal isn't to be perfect—it's to elevate others beyond where you are.

ACTION STEP: Identify one person you can mentor intentionally for the next 90 days. Focus on what will make them independent, not dependent. Ask yourself: "If I disappeared tomorrow, could they lead without me?"

2. THE LET-GO AUDIT

TOOL: Review your top performers. Are you helping them grow—or holding them back? Sometimes love means opening the door, not keeping people close.

ACTION STEP: For each top performer, ask: "If they left tomorrow, would I be proud—or resentful?" If it's the latter, start preparing them for flight. Celebrate their next opportunity, even if it means losing them from your team.

3. THE INVISIBLE LEADERSHIP TEST

TOOL: Lead a project without broadcasting that you're leading it. Create conditions for success, then step back and let the team take ownership.

ACTION STEP: Empower your team to make decisions and drive outcomes. If they succeed and say, "We did it ourselves," you've passed the test. That's the highest form of leadership.

4. THE LEGACY LENS EXERCISE

TOOL: Project yourself 10 years ahead. Imagine your mentees, your team, or your family looking back. What do you hope they remember about how you led them?

ACTION STEP: Write down what you hope they'll say you taught them—and how you made them feel. Not what you accomplished, but what you helped them become. Revisit this quarterly to stay aligned with your vision of your legacy.

5. THE CULTURE-BUILDER FRAMEWORK

TOOL: Identify the difference between an excellent culture (dependent on you) and a culture of excellence (sustainable without you). Document the values, systems, and principles that should outlast your presence.

ACTION STEP: Write down your team's core values and the stories behind them. Share why you do things, not just how. If you left today, would people know why your culture exists—or would it disappear with you?

6. THE UNCONTAINED VISION STATEMENT

TOOL: Write a personal statement of leadership purpose that has no expiration date. This isn't a career goal—it's a life mission that transcends any single role or season.

ACTION STEP: Complete this sentence: "I lead so that…" Write it down. Revisit it every year. If it still holds true, you're on the right path. If it's changed, ask yourself why—and adjust your leadership accordingly.

Quick Reference: The Legacy Checklist

Ask yourself weekly:

- Who did I invest in this week?
- What did I teach that can be replicated?
- Where did I step back and let someone else lead?
- What will remain if I leave tomorrow?

Ask yourself quarterly:

- Am I creating followers, or leaders?
- Have I released anyone who was ready to fly?
- Is my culture dependent on me, or sustainable without me?

Reflection

Leadership, at its highest form, is not about being remembered for what you did.

It's about being remembered for what you made possible.

If your influence continues to shape lives long after you've stepped away, then your life—and your leadership—were never contained.

FINAL WORD

I started this journey as a kid who lost his father, burned his furniture to stay warm, ran from structure, ran toward violence, and somehow—through grace, faith, grit, and a few miracles—found purpose in leading others.

If my life says anything, I hope it says this:

You can be uncontained—by circumstance, by labels, by expectations—and still be grounded in purpose.

You can lead with strength and still be guided by faith.

You can build something that outlives you—not because your name is on it, but because your fingerprints are on people.

Leadership isn't about how brightly you burn. It's about what light remains when you're gone.

THE WAY FORWARD

As you close this book and return to your leadership challenges, remember Bruce Lee's philosophy:

Absorb what is useful. Discard what is not. Add what is uniquely your own.

Take the frameworks, stories, and tools from these pages and blend them with your own experience, your own values, and your own authentic style. Don't try to lead like Martin White or like Bruce Lee—lead like the best version of yourself.

The world needs leaders who can adapt, who can learn, who can stay curious and humble even as they grow in influence and responsibility. It needs leaders who are Outboxed—uncontained by convention, unlimited by tradition, and unafraid to keep evolving.

Your leadership journey is unique, but the principles are universal:

- Stay adaptive
- Stay learning
- Always remember that the goal isn't to create followers—it's to create more leaders

**That's how you change the world.
One adaptive leader at a time.**

FINAL ADDITIONS & A SNEAK PEEK

COMING SOON FROM MARTIN WHITE

If leadership in the workplace builds influence, leadership at home builds legacy.

In my next book, I'll be exploring the other side of the leadership coin—the one that matters most. Because no promotion, no title, and no professional achievement mean anything if it costs you the people you love.

At the time of writing *Outboxed*, I've been married for thirty-five years to my beautiful wife, Sue. We met at nineteen, married at twenty, and—as they say—the rest is history. Through every deployment, transition, and reinvention, she was the one constant voice telling me the truth, whether I wanted to hear it or not.

And then there were my daughters—Ariel and Ashia. Raising them felt like raising two only children, each with their own season and rhythm. They taught me patience, resilience, and the power of showing up when it mattered most.

MARRIAGE, FAMILY, AND THE LEADERSHIP THAT MATTERS MOST

My upcoming book dives deep into the lessons that shaped my life outside of uniform and titles:

- Marriage isn't 50/50—it's whatever's required in the moment. Sometimes it's 90/10, and that's not imbalance—that's partnership.
- Your spouse isn't just your supporter—they're your Chief Operating Officer, creating the conditions for your success.
- Work-life balance is seasonal. The key isn't perfection—it's knowing when to recalibrate.
- Presence matters more than provision. Your kids won't remember your paycheck—they'll remember whether you showed up.
- Leadership at home isn't about titles or authority—it's about partnership, presence, and perspective.

In this next book, I'll share:

- The PARTNER Framework—seven principles for family-supported leadership
- The 90/10 Rule of Seasons—how to navigate imbalance without losing your family
- Practical tools like the Weekly Check-In, Work-Life Calibration Tool, and the Legacy Ledger
- Real stories of deployment, absence, reinvention, and how my family carried me through it all

THE WEIGHT OF THE HOMEFRONT

During my years in the Navy, I deployed often. I would come and go with the mission, but Sue held the line at home. She made sure the kids were safe, the finances were steady, and our household was intact. That stability was a gift—because while I was out at sea, I could focus on the mission knowing the homefront was strong.

The real challenge came after I retired. For more than two decades, our rhythm was my leaving and her running the show. Suddenly, I was home every day. For most families, that's normal. For us, it was a shift that took some getting used to.

Sue gave me the space to chase the man I wanted to become, while keeping me tethered to the man I already was—a husband, a father, and a partner.

A LEGACY BUILT AT HOME

Ariel, born when I was twenty-one, grew up with the Navy version of me—the sailor who was always gone, the father chasing deployments. She taught me patience and the power of showing up when I could.

Ashia, born eight years later, got a different version of me—still military, but older, wiser, more aware of the cost of absence. Together, my daughters grounded me in the truth that no career means anything if it costs you the people you love most.

This next book isn't just about my family—it's about yours. It's about the leadership that happens when the uniform comes off, when the title doesn't matter, and when the only thing that counts is whether you're present.

Because if the workplace is where you build influence, the home is where you build legacy.

A strong family doesn't just support a leader—it creates one.

Stay tuned for more...

CALL TO ACTION

If you're ready to **build differently** and **lead differently**, connect with me.

Scan the QR code and join my leadership network.

www.ingramcontent.com/pod-product-compliance
Lightning Source LLC
Chambersburg PA
CBHW060352190426
43201CB00044B/2099